A Brief History of British

Mountaineering

A Brief History of British

Mountaineering

by **Colin Wells** for **The Mountain Heritage Trust**

with a foreword by **Sir Chris Bonington**, CBE

Published by **The Mountain Heritage Trust**

Designed, typeset and produced by **Vertebrate Graphics**, Sheffield.
Printed and bound by Clearpoint Colourprint, Nottingham.

Acknowledgements

This attempt at a 'sampler' of British mountaineering history has been a collaborative effort
involving many people, but the Mountain Heritage Trust would particularly like to thank
the following: Colin Wells the author, the editorial and design staff of Vertebrate Graphics;
Sir Chris Bonington, Derek Walker and Audrey Salkeld for their invaluable and insightful
comments and corrections to the text; Steve Bell, Ian Smith, Andy MacNae and the
MHT Committee for further suggestions and, in particular, all the photographers who
have generously allowed us to use their photographs.

Thanks are also due to a vast cast of mountaineering historians, past and present, who have
provided the written material on which this little book has freely drawn; in particular, the many
excellent books and articles written by those outstanding researchers of British mountaineering
history, Sir Chris Bonington, Alan Hankinson, Audrey Salkeld, Walt Unsworth and Ken Wilson.

Contents

Foreword by Sir **Chris Bonington**, CBE VII

1 **Origins** **1**

2 The **Playground** of **Europe**
(1850–1900) **5**
- Edward Whymper & the epic of the Matterhorn (1865)
- Women alpinists
- The Alps

3 **On** the **Rock**
(1880–1914) **15**
- The Abraham Brothers
- John Collie (1859–1942)
- The evolution of climbing equipment 1

4 The **Great** Game
Exploring the mountains of the Caucasus,
the Americas and the Greater Ranges of Asia
(1870–1910) **23**
- The road to K2 (1882–1893)
- Aleister Crowley (1875–1947)
- Dr Alexander Kellas (1868–1921)

5 **Discovering Everest**
(1850–1924) **31**
- George Mallory (1886–1924)
- 'English air' Early attempts at using bottled oxygen
- Vanquishing none but ourselves
  The epic of Mallory & Irvine (1924)
- Andrew 'Sandy' Irvine (1902–1924)

6 **Hidden Himalaya**
(1930–1939) **41**
- Eric Shipton (1907–1977)
  Keeping it simple
- Bill Tilman (1898–1977)
  Adventure ahoy!
- The Karakoram

7 **Regaining** the **Heights**
(1920–1940) **49**
- Sid Cross (1913–1998)
- Alice Nelson (1911–)
- Colin Kirkus (1910–1940)
- The evolution of climbing equipment 2
- Aid (Artificial) Climbing

8 **Climbing Everest**
(1933–1953) **59**
- Frank Smythe (1900–1949)
- 'All this and Everest too!'
  The New Elizabethans triumph at last (1953)
- Sir Edmund Hillary (1919–)

9 The **Cragrats**
Post-war British climbing
(1945–1970) **69**
- The Baron – Joe Brown (1930–)
- The Villain – Don Whillans (1933–1985)
- Tom Patey (1932–1970)
- The evolution of climbing equipment 3
- Television & climbing

10 From **Himalayan** Circus to Alpine **Style**
(1955–) **79**
- Joe Tasker (1948–1982)
- Pete Boardman (1950–1982)
- Sir Chris Bonington, CBE (1934–)
- Triumph & tragedy
  Tales from the edge of endurance
- Doug Scott (1941–)
- Mick Fowler
  'The Mountaineers' Mountaineer' (1956–)

11 **Modern** Times
British climbing in the late 20th Century
(1970–) **91**
- The evolution of climbing equipment 4
- Paul Pritchard (1967–)
- Leo Houlding (1980–)

12 **Mountain** Peoples **101**
- Nepal Himalaya
  Sherpas, Tamangs, Rais and others
- Tenzing Norgay Sherpa (1914–1986)
- Baltis and Hunzakuts
  The indigenous mountaineers of the Karakoram
- Nazir Sabir (1955–)

Photo Credits **117**

Index **118**

Foreword by
Sir **Chris Bonington**, CBE

Britain's Mountain Heritage is especially rich. It is one of the oldest in the world and, almost from the beginning, reached out from our small hills and crags to the greater ranges of the Alps and the world's highest mountains. This book tells the story of our sport from the first recorded climb – Coleridge's descent of *Broad Stand* in the early nineteenth century – to the present day. It captures the extraordinary range of personalities that mountaineering has spawned. It is no coincidence that of all sports, climbing has the richest and most varied literature.

This book represents much more than a memento of Britain's first *National Mountaineering Exhibition*. It provides a full, very readable record of the way our sport has developed over the years, from the early days – when climbers used a short length of hemp rope, were clad in their knee breeches and Norfolk jackets, and wore a pair of nailed boots on their feet – up to the present day, with its array of high-tech camming devices, sticky rubber, high-performance fabrics and sophisticated training routines.

Yet, in watching the videos in the exhibition of earlier climbers and the modern young hot-shots, and listening to them talk of their aspirations and attitudes, there is a common theme, also picked up in this book, that is the constant quest for the unknown – of extending the boundaries of what seems possible, of using whatever technology has been developed, not simply to make the climbing safer, but to go further and ever more boldly. There is also an underlying theme of fun, of zany humour and irreverence that is an important part of our heritage.

You can see the ongoing conflict between our desire to survive and the need to play out the game of risk, both in the book and the exhibition. In modern climbing, it can be seen in the dichotomy between sport climbing, where the use of expansion bolts minimises the element of danger to enable the climber to concentrate on the purely athletic side of the sport, and adventure climbing, where he or she accepts the rock as it is, places protection when possible in cracks and crannies, and embraces the element of risk as something central to the activity.

What also comes out both in the book and in the exhibition, is the importance of the beauty of the environment in which we climb.

Whether you are a dedicated climber or someone who enjoys our hills and mountains from the valleys, I believe this book will extend your understanding of our mountain heritage.

Chris Bonington, 2001

Origins

The farther I ascend from animated Nature, from men, and cattle, and the common birds of the woods and fields, the greater becomes in me the Intensity of the feeling of Life.

Samuel Taylor Coleridge

The threat of a heavy shower was hanging in the air as a chubby-faced man gingerly picked his way down the rock-strewn slopes of **Scafell** (963m). A strong wind was blowing billowing clouds of cumulus from the Irish Sea towards the Lakeland mountains, and yet the air still possessed sufficient clarity to view the neighbouring peaks for 80km around. However, Samuel Taylor Coleridge, leading light of the romantic movement, was at that moment focusing on a piece of mountain landscape a little closer to hand. He had reached a series of steep rocky steps, each successively trickier to descend and dangerously poised over a fearful drop. 'There is one sort of gambling to which I am much addicted', Coleridge would later explain, 'When I find it convenient to descend from a mountain, I am too confident and too indolent to look round about and wind about 'till I find a track or other symptom of safety; but I wander on... relying on fortune.' He steadied himself above the steepest bit of rock, flung his fell pole down the cliff in a flamboyant gesture of commitment and began to lower himself over the little abyss by his finger ends, boots scrabbling for unseen holds below. 'Every drop increased the Palsy of my Limbs – I shook all over.' But Coleridge kept his cool and made it to the safety of *Mickledore Col* below where, 'I lay in a state of almost prophetic Trance and Delight – and blessed God aloud, for the powers of Reason and Will, which remaining no Danger can overpower us!' Coleridge was clearly experiencing the first ever climber's endorphin rush, which was not unexpected: he had just made Britain's first recorded rock climb. It was August 5th, 1802 and he'd just descended *Broad Stand*.

It was perhaps inevitable that the first person to get intimately acquainted with the rockface was a romantic poet. Ever since the leading lyricist of the day, Thomas Gray, had started idealising the Lakeland landscape in 1769 as akin to 'Elysium' in places, and mesmerisingly 'Gothick' in others, it had attracted the creative community to visit and, in some cases, stay. It was only a matter of time before residents like Wordsworth and Coleridge began exploring the high fells and, in the latter's case, allowed their boldness to extend to clambering about on or near precipices. Coleridge may have possessed an addictive personality, but the buzz he got from scrambling near big drops seemed to top any opium high. His description of the feeling of exhilaration is recognisable to any modern mountaineer: 'I have always found this *stretched and anxious* state of mind favourable to depth of pleasurable Impression, in the resting places and *lownding* Coves'.

But this embrace of wilderness as something exquisite rather than execrable was a sudden change in fashion. For centuries, the rough crags and moors of Britain's uplands had been regarded from a purely utilitarian perspective. At best, they were useless wasteland, and at worst, positively dangerous. Until the mid-18th century the idea of visiting upland areas like the Lake District for pleasure would have been regarded as preposterous. Daniel Defoe, for example, passing by in 1723 on his *Tour through the whole Island of Great Britain*, found that 'These hills had a kind of inhospitable terror in them...all barren and wild, of no use or advantage either to man or beast.' Even as late as 1773, Dr Samuel Johnson summarily dismissed the mountains: 'An eye accustomed to flowering pastures and waving harvests is astonished and repelled by this wide extent of hopeless sterility.'

The change to modern perspectives, of regarding mountains as magnificent rather than maudlin, was encouraged by the propaganda pictures of two artists, William Bellers and Thomas Smith, who went to Keswick in the mid-18th century to paint what they saw. The first conjured up images of restful pastoral quietude, while the latter saw dramatic jagged cliffs and thunderclouds. Both were exaggerated approximations of the truth, but both opened the eyes of the wealthy, educated population to an area of picturesque wild country of which they had been mostly ignorant. The scribblers quickly followed in the wake of the picturemakers and began extolling the Arcadian beauties of the region. It was only a matter of time before the first curious visitors arrived, since when the Lake District tourist industry has never looked back.

From the ranks of the new tourists sprang the first of the fellwalkers. One of the most notable of these early mountain climbers was retired army captain Joseph Budworth, who had lost an arm during the siege of Gibraltar, but who retained an undiminished zest for life. In 1792 he covered more than 380km in just two weeks, hiring local guides to take him into the high fells. When he publicised his escapades in a book, a trend was set and fellwalking started to grow as a respectable and fashionable pastime. In other areas, such as Snowdonia, incursions into the mountains were also beginning, but sprang from a different imperative than that of aesthetic appreciation or mere fashion: science. When William Bingley, a Cambridge undergraduate, scouted the cliffs and ledges of

Samuel Taylor Coleridge

James Forbes

Snowdon (1,085m) in 1798 in the company of Llanberis Rector Peter Williams, it was in the search for botanical riches, rather than spiritual beatitudes. And it was also under the guise of science that the first probings by the British into the Alpine arena began.

Britain, in the course of expanding its global empire had acquired the habit of exploration in wild and woolly parts of the world and had consequently developed a tradition of geographical inquiry, which was serviced by the universities and academics. Partly as a result of this tradition, Britain had become a leading nation in the study of Geological Sciences and during the early nineteenth century, one of the outstanding questions facing the discipline was the nature and behaviour of glaciers. One of the figures wrestling with this problem was the Scotsman, James Forbes. A Professor of Natural Philosophy at Edinburgh University, he spent a considerable amount of time between 1835 and 1842 travelling, climbing and studying in the Alps, observing and collecting evidence for his theory of glacier movement. Some of his climbs, however, had little scientific justification, and were purely adventurous, such as his ascent of the **Jungfrau** (4,158m) in 1841. In 1842 he spent much of the summer on the Mer de Glace above Chamonix in order to gain an intimate insight into the working of a great glacier. This culminated in his ground-breaking work which became known as the 'Viscous Theory' which first proposed that glacier ice did not behave like a solid at all, as everyone had assumed, but more like a very slowly deforming liquid. Forbes's influence in pump-priming the imminent invasion of the Alps by British climbers lay not so much in his scientific discoveries, but in his descriptions of the climbs he had made

there. The prevailing orthodoxy was that the pursuit of scientific knowledge was the only noble reason for venturing high, his semi-autobiographical book, *Travels through the Alps*, actually contained rather a lot of uninhibited high adventure. H.D. Inglis wrote in 1833 that:

> *"It is a positive act of egregious folly for one not moved by scientific motives to endure the pain and danger of an ascent greatly above the line of perpetual congelation",*

but by 1843 the scientist, Forbes, was writing racily about gripping battles with bergschrunds high on sheer mountain tops. These accounts, along with self-penned sketches of the mountains, captured the imagination of a public thirsty for new areas to visit and marvel at. The success of the publicity afforded to the Alps was such that thirty years later, Sir George Airy, the Astronomer Royal, was to bemoan the fact: 'I suppose it may be asserted that the present popularity of Zermatt, a place which was before scarcely known, is almost entirely due to Professor Forbes's picture of the Matterhorn'.

Forbes's perhaps inadvertent promotion of the Alps was joined by that of artist and social reformer John Ruskin who cut through the soft-focus haze generated by the Romantics to extol the beauty of the geological form beneath. He advocated a different aesthetic appreciation of mountains based on scientific principles, but unlike the corrupted glaciologists, he abhorred the concept of mountaineering for fun. 'True lovers of natural beauty', he declaimed with almost Cromwellian fervour, 'would as soon think of climbing the pillars of the choir at Beauvais for a gymnastic exercise, as of making a playground of Alpine snow'. Ironically, his

writings about the Alps had quite the opposite effect, encouraging a much greater awareness of the superb mountains lying across the Channel, and inculcating a latent desire to climb up them.

One of the early 'mountain tourists' to take up the challenge was one Albert Smith. An erstwhile surgeon from Chertsey, he had become enamoured of the idea of climbing **Mont Blanc** (4,807m) when a child. Mont Blanc had exercised a fascination over many continental scientists ever since it was discovered that it was the highest peak in western Europe. Genevan scientist Horace-Benedict de Saussure had offered a cash prize in 1760 to encourage the first ascent but, despite many unsuccessful attempts by would-be mountaineering bounty hunters, it was not actually climbed until 1786 by Dr Paccard and Jacques Balmat. Over the

Albert Smith, 'The Barnum of Mont Blanc'

ensuing decades the ascent had lost none of its cachet as a feat of great scientific endeavour (early parties were invariably encumbered with aneroid barometers, telescopes, notebooks and other sundry scientific paraphernalia) and returning summiteers were fêted as heroes by the townsfolk of Chamonix. Although it is undeniably the highest mountain in the Alps, Mont Blanc is also one of the most straightforward to climb, comprising mostly easy-angled snow slopes. The greatest danger came from the weather, crevasses and avalanches, and it wasn't until 1820 that anyone suffered any serious mishap on the mountain. In that year Dr Hamel, a Russian scientist, tried to climb Mont Blanc with a view to observing the effect of rarefied air upon animal organisms (he carried baskets containing homing pigeons intending to see whether they could fly in thin air). Before he could conduct his ornithological experiments, his party unfortunately observed another interesting natural phenomenon at close quarters as they became the first climbers to be avalanched. Although eight members of the party survived, three guides lost their lives. The story of the accident was a minor sensation in England, as the party had included two Oxford students.

Smith had read about the epic of Hamel and his party and been captivated by the notion of battling up the fearsome snows of the roof of Europe. He had been moved to construct a small animated panorama depicting the Hamel ascent, with which he frightened his little sister while re-enacting the disastrous events of 1820 – a skill, which he would put to good use in adult life. While studying in Paris in 1835, Smith seized the opportunity to visit Chamonix but was unable to climb his obsession, Mont Blanc, due to his penurious state as a medical

student. He even tried hitching a lift as a porter, but no one seemed to be trying their luck on the mountain that season. Back in Chertsey practicing medicine, Smith's thoughts often wandered back to the gleaming heights of the Alps, and to assuage his longing and to amuse the local literary societies, he devised a show depicting the ascent of Mont Blanc which was on a more ambitious scale than his childhood prototype. The shows went down very well: he had unwittingly found his true *métier* – an ability to entertain.

Moving to London in 1841, Smith soon abandoned surgery when he found he could make a living writing amusing pieces for the likes of *Punch* and turning out polished sketches, plays, novels and, most importantly, pantomime. He expanded into travel writing, visiting Egypt and Turkey and developed a stage show based on his book of travels. This gave him an idea. He had not forgotten his boyhood ambition to climb Mont Blanc and in 1851, he determined to fulfil it at last. On August 12th he staggered up the mountain along with three bemused Oxford undergraduates and guides laden with 91 bottles of wine, three bottles of Cognac, numerous loaves and manifold cheeses, chocolates, bags of sugar, legs of mutton and 46 fowls. And that was before breakfast. The ascent occurred without incident (apart from Smith unsurprisingly falling asleep on the summit) and marked the 40th successful ascent of the mountain. What made it significant was how Smith exploited his experience. He concocted an entertainment called *The Ascent of Mont Blanc* and hired Piccadilly's Egyptian Hall to stage it in. It opened in March 1852 and ran without a break for seven years. The show comprised Smith narrating the history of the

mountain and his climb against a background of rolling paintings illuminated from behind. In order to spice up the patter, Smith interspersed the chat with songs, jokes, and employed showgirls dressed as Alpine maidens parading great St Bernard Dogs. It was mountaineering music hall. In the words of climbing historian Walt Unsworth, Smith was 'The Barnum of Mont Blanc'. The show may not have been on the same cerebral plane as Forbes and Ruskin, but it certainly put bums on seats and put Mont Blanc on the map. Now everyone knew about the Alps and what fun it was to climb them.

Thus, by the middle of the nineteenth century two strands of intellectual endeavour, science and art, had combined with a third, baser human instinct – commercial exploitation – to produce the conditions necessary for the mass participation of the British in Alpine mountaineering. This was to result in an unprecedented orgy of peak-bagging in the following decade and a half: a period dubbed 'The Golden Age' of Alpine climbing.

Top: Smith giving one of his magic lantern shows at London's Egyptian Hall

Above: Advertisement for Smith's twice-weekly shows

The
Playground
of Europe

(1850–1900)

The knapsack of Alpine lore is closing; and can we venture to assert that they who pack it leave one small corner unoccupied?

Edward Shirley Kennedy, 1855

Left: The **Matterhorn** (4,478m), seen from the east, reflected in the Riffelsee

The **Golden Age** (1850–1865)

A critical mass in the numbers of people interested in mountaineering for pleasure and sporting achievement had been reached by the middle of the 19th century. The following decade and a half would see most of the major Alpine mountains climbed, largely by wealthy Englishmen and their local guides. This period of frenetic activity became known as the Golden Age of Alpine climbing. A few adventurous souls like John Hudson and Thomas Kennedy occasionally climbed without guides, but most of the mountains were ascended thanks to a symbiotic relationship between members of the Alpine Club and a small élite of indigenous local mountain experts. It was generally the guides that selected the line to follow up a mountain and undertook the heavy labour of cutting steps in snow and ice. The clients may have called the shots when it came to selecting the mountain to climb, but they nearly always deferred to the judgement of their guide. '*Mein Herr*, you are the master in the valley,' Oberland guide Peter Bohren is famously reported as saying to a English client, 'but I am master here.' Even so, the standard of climbing ability among the guides was remarkably low. Because of this, the few outstanding ones, such as Bohren, Michel Croz and Melchior Anderegg became greatly sought-after celebrities in their own right.

Accomplished intellectuals like the literary critic Leslie Stephen, scientist John Tyndall and senior civil servant Adolphus Moore were among the many key players who became the founding fathers of a new sport. It was perhaps inevitable, therefore, that it was not long before the idea of a club for Alpine climbers should be formed in order that gentlemen could meet and discuss their activities, pass on information and generally network in the time-honoured way of élite groupings. The 'Alpine Club' held its first meeting in London just before Christmas 1857. The initial concept of an informal dining club was soon superseded by a much grander notion of a semi-professional association with regular meetings to discuss papers relating to mountain exploration. Within two years it was

Outside the Club Room of Zermatt, in 1864   *Etching by Edward Whymper*

Thomas Kennedy

Melchior Anderegg

publishing them and by 1863 this had evolved into a regular journal. The Alpine Club was a dominant influence on the early development of the sport and its tastes and decrees established the orthodoxies which affected all climbers – a position which was to result in its becoming complacent and out of touch with modern climbing later in the century. In the meantime, it played a major part in driving forward the mania to climb as many Alpine summits as possible in the shortest possible time. 1865 is generally held to mark the end of this Golden Age. The year marked the apogee of peak-bagging: more new summits were climbed that summer than any before or since.

But there was also another event which emphatically book-ended the era – the incident-packed ascent of that most spectacular of Alpine peaks: the Matterhorn.

The Matterhorn (4,478m)

After Everest, the Matterhorn is probably the most famous mountain in the world. A 4,478m rock pyramid with an outline exhibiting a rough symmetry, it represents the very idealised picture of a mountain that a child might draw. As a consequence, its picturesque image adorns placemats, key fobs, biscuit tins and paperweights and has even proved the inspiration for a well-known brand of Swiss confectionery. Split between Italy and Switzerland, the mountain has four faces and ridges, the easiest of which is the *North East (Hörnli) Ridge*, the line taken on the original ascent. The popularity of the mountain shows no signs of abating; it is estimated that around 3,000 climbers a year make the pilgrimage to its historic summit.

Edward Whymper
& the epic *of the*
Matterhorn (1865)

Ascent of the Matterhorn July 14th 1865 by Lord Francis Douglas, Hudson, Hadow, & Whymper + 3 guides

The climbing of the **Matterhorn** (4,479m) was a story of high drama which precipitated a mountaineering media story of global interest. It contained a combination of dangerous adventure and human interest which journalists found irresistible. There was courage, naked ambition, treachery, nationalist rivalry, triumph, emotion, blunders and ultimately death. It was the sensation of 1865.

The build-up to the momentous events began with the ambitions of Edward Whymper, a wood-engraving illustrator from London. Whymper had a secret dream. Impressed by the glorious adventures of the Royal Navy's polar exploration, which were all the talk of the chattering classes, he too desired to become a national hero in the mould of a James Ross or John Franklin. He wrote:

"I had ideas floating in my head that I should one day turn out some great person."

When he was offered a commission to visit the Alps to draw book illustrations, he leapt at the chance, thinking it might enable him to become familiar with the properties of snow and ice. But on arriving in the mountains that summer of 1860, he immediately recognised that mountaineering in Switzerland might offer a more direct route to celebrity than polar exploration. The following season, aged just 22 and with no prior mountaineering experience, he returned to make the first British ascent of **Mont Pelvoux** (4,103m) and his first attempt on the Matterhorn. He immediately tilted at the latter for the prime reason that it was one of the two highest unclimbed peaks left in Alps – and he knew that conquering it would be a major challenge and give him recognition as a great mountaineer. The other, the **Weisshorn** (4,506m), was climbed that year by Irish scientist John Tyndall – who would become one of Whymper's rivals for the prize of the Matterhorn. Already, the elements of a great battle were in

Charles Hudson

Lord Francis Douglas

Michel Croz

place. But there were good reasons why the Matterhorn remained unclimbed. The 4,479m peak, which bestrode the Swiss/Italian border, was defended on three sides by steep ridges of rock which looked impregnable. Prior to Whymper's failed initial foray onto the Italian side, there had been few attempts – Tyndall being one of those to reconnoitre the fearsome peak.

He returned for more the following summer, but was beaten back by storm. Down in the valley, he met the local Italian Jean-Anthoine Carrel, who had been attracted to Whymper's hotel by rumours that an Englishman was trying to climb the mountain. Carrel, a war veteran of the Austro-Italian war of independence was intensely patriotic. He secretly felt that the Matterhorn was not only his personal preserve, but that as half of it lay in Italy, it should be climbed from that side by an Italian. Although more of an ex-soldier than a guide, he had already made a couple of attempts himself. Perhaps sensing in him a similar driven ambition, Whymper took an instant liking to Carrel's rough-hewn character. In 1862 and 1863 they joined forces to make several unsuccessful attempts on the mountain. Carrel was also present as a porter in 1862 when Tyndall made an attempt; almost making it to the top before his guides cautioned retreat. (There was later speculation that Carrel may have helped influence the decision to go back because he secretly wanted to be in charge of the successful party.) The following seasons of 1864 and 1865 saw Whymper flowering as a mountaineer, climbing a total of over 30,000m and covering nearly 650km in just one month alone in 1865. With other Alpine Club members and guides, he knocked off a series of major first ascents, and also had another crack at the Matterhorn by its

stonefall-prone *East Face*. He retreated under heavy bombardment, provoking the question from one his guides: 'Why don't you try to go up a mountain which *can* be ascended?' But Whymper was undeterred and the Greek Tragedy of the final assault was inevitable.

A series of bizarre coincidences led up to the events of 1865. The Italian Alpine Club had been founded two years earlier, thanks to efforts of the Italian Minister of Finance, Quintino Sella. He decided that its foundation should be marked by a prestigious mountaineering achievement. What could be better than the conquest of the mighty Matterhorn, half of which was Italian territory? Sella sent for Carrel, the acknowledged Italian expert on the mountain, who was in turn overjoyed by the thought of guiding a party of his countrymen to the summit without having to play second fiddle to some rich foreigner. The planning was to be undertaken in secret, and Carrel was sworn to silence. Unfortunately, Carrel had also agreed to help Whymper with an attempt on the mountain. He got out of this corner by soft-flannelling Whymper with a story about having to honour an engagement to escort a 'family of distinction' in the valley of Aosta.

Whymper was put out, but this was nothing compared to what he felt when he discovered that Carrel had in fact gone to join an Italian party to tackle the Matterhorn. Outraged by what he regarded as treachery, Whymper cast about desperately for a means to climb the mountain without Carrel's assistance. This was not made easier by the fact that the Italians were deliberately attempting to stall Whymper's attempt. The nominated leader of the Italian Matterhorn party, Felice Giordino warned Sella: 'I have tried to keep everything a secret but that

Jean-Anthoine Carrel

fellow, whose life seems to depend on the Matterhorn, is here suspiciously prying into everything. I have taken all the competent men away from him and yet he is so enamoured of this mountain that he may go up with others and make a scene.' Giordino was right. Whymper was in such a state, that if a donkey had walked into his hotel and offered to accompany him up the mountain he would probably have gone. As luck would have it, it was not a donkey, but the 19-year old rising star of the Alpine Club, Lord Francis Douglas and his guides, 'Old' Peter and 'Young' Peter Taugwalder. Whymper rapidly persuaded them to return to Zermatt to try the most intimidating unclimbed peak in the Alps from the Swiss side. The team swelled further when they bumped into the great guide Michel Croz who had climbed with Whymper earlier in the season. He had already been engaged by the experienced English alpinist Charles Hudson – for an attempt on the Matterhorn! Now they were six – which rapidly became seven. As part of the deal to join forces, Hudson insisted that a young friend of his accompany them: the inexperienced novice climber Douglas Hadow. This was to prove the party's ultimate downfall.

raced up the final snow slopes fearful that the Italians might have beaten him to his cherished career pinnacle. He breathed a huge sigh of relief when he spotted Carrel's party down on the *Italian Ridge*, still 400m from the summit. With great triumphal whooping and the hurling of stones, Whymper's party made it known in no uncertain terms that the Italians were beaten. Carrel looked up in despair and abandoned the climb.

But that was to be the last joyful moment of the climb for the successful team. Roped together on the tricky descent, the hopelessly inexperienced Hadow slipped, pulling with him three of the others. The last in line, who were tied to the rest of the chain by a weak sash-cord which broke under the strain, could only gape aghast as one of the most famous guides in the Alps, an English Lord, an accomplished English climber and an unfortunate novice, plummeted to their deaths. Their fall was watched in horror by the survivors, Edward Whymper and the Taugwalders.

'Is it life? Is it duty? Is it common sense? Is it allowable? Is it not wrong?' babbled *The Times* in shocked reaction to news of the disaster. It characterised the hysterical reaction of the press to the event, and meant that overnight Whymper became the most famous and notorious mountaineer in the world.

On the perfectly clear morning of July 13th the unwieldy party set off in pursuit of the prize from Zermatt on Whymper's ninth attempt. There were four climbers of vastly different experience and three guides speaking two different languages. Despite the oddball mix and communication problems they made rapid progress up the Swiss *Hörnli Ridge*, camping part-way up.

The next morning they overcame the long-feared upper section comparatively easily: it was much less difficult than it looked. Whymper

Peter Taugwalder (Sohn)

Edward Whymper

Peter Taugwalder (Vater)

The SURVIVORS

Below: The sash cord with which the elder Taugwalder connected himself, his son and Whymper to the others

Lord Francis Douglas

Charles Hudson

Michel Croz

Douglas Hadow

The FATALITIES

Women
alpinists

Although women had been present at the very earliest stages of mountain climbing, the first steps could be classified very much in the 'stunt' category.

Maria Paradis, who was dragged up **Mont Blanc** (4,807m) by guides in 1808, undertook the ascent more to promote her Chamonix refreshment stall, than from a burning desire to get to the summit. She never climbed another mountain.

The first woman to gain the summit unaided was a very different kettle of fish. Henriette d'Angeville bagged 'the Blanc' in 1838 and has strong claims to be the first genuine female mountaineer. She continued her climbing career until she was 69 when she retired, declaring: 'It is wise at my age to drop the alpenstock before the alpenstock drops me'.

But it was Britons who began to set the pace of emancipated alpinism. The first British female to top Mont Blanc was Mrs Hamilton in 1854, but more significant was the first winter ascent of the mountain by either gender, a feat achieved by Isabella Straton and three Chamonix guides in 1876. Lucy Walker, meanwhile, had been climbing difficult Alps since 1864 in the company of family members and in 1871 made the first female ascent of the **Matterhorn** (4,478m).

From then on, more and more women joined in the peak-bagging frenzy, proving tougher and more competitive than many of the men. Katy Richardson was a case in point; she made 116 major climbs of which six were first ascents and 14 first women's ascents. The Pidgeon sisters (Anna and Ellen) traversed the Matterhorn, toughing it out against storms and bivouacking on the *Hörnli Ridge*. Lizzie le Blond, another great pioneer started climbing as an all-female rope (many women had previously climbed with husbands or male guides and friends) famously traversing the **Piz Palu** (3,908m) with Lady Evelyn McDonnell.

Women climbers had to contend with more than just snowstorms, rockfalls and avalanches however;

there was also the extra hurdle of male prejudice. The Alpine Club would not countenance female members, so in 1907 the women defiantly started their own version – the Ladies Alpine Club.

Starchy Victorian dress codes added to the lady-alpinist's burden. Although some women achieved extraordinary mountaineering feats wearing long skirts, many wore jodhpurs underneath, removing their skirts once well out of sight of the valleys. A few radical souls like Mary Paillon, simply wore men's clothes. As the century progressed, women climbers triumphed over barriers both physical and social.

One of the outstanding new breed of female alpinists of the late nineteenth century was Lily Bristow. She became famous when in 1892, along with a French female climber, she became the first women to ascend the **Charmoz** (3,445m) as part of a team led by A.F. Mummery. Bristow went on to take part in difficult climbs on the **Dru** (3,754m), **Zinalrothorn** (4,221m), **Matterhorn** (4,479m) and the second-ever traverse of the **Grépon** (3,482m). It was this performance that prompted Mummery's famous quip about the revered route being 'an easy day for a lady'. But Bristow was clearly no ordinary lady; she represented the vanguard of an army of skillful women climbers which would continue to grow throughout the 20th century.

Above: Lizzie le Blond wearing the kind of mask that lady alpinists wore to avoid turning a vulgar brown in the Alpine sun

Going guideless:
Mummery
& the birth of modern alpinism
(1880–1895)

A.F. Mummery

The Matterhorn accident put a damper on Alpine climbing for quite a while. In later years the US climber William Coolidge recollected vividly, 'the sort of palsy that fell upon the good cause of that frightful catastrophe', particularly amongst English climbers. They went about under a sort of dark shade, looked on with scarcely disguised contempt by ordinary travellers. They climbed on sufferance, enjoying themselves much, it is true, but keeping all expression of that joy to themselves in order not to excite derision.

Climbing went underground. The purdah was broken in 1871, however, with the publication of Edward Whymper's semi-autobiographical *Scrambles Amongst the Alps* and Leslie Stephen's elegantly witty climbing reminiscences: *The Playground of Europe.* The books helped revive mass interest in climbing following its period in the public doghouse.

In the post-Matterhorn era, things were changing. Until then the accepted wisdom was that no amateur climber could ever hope to match the proficiency of the guide (in the first flush of Darwinian enthusiasm, Alpine Club member George Wherry even tried to prove that guides had evolved specially adapted feet). By the later stages of the century, however, the view was becoming outmoded and restricted to a few die-hard traditionalists.

The new breed of climber would find less need for guides. With most of the major Alpine peaks climbed by 1870, he (or she, for more women were at last beginning to enter the Alpine arena) was more interested in the way to the summit, rather than the summit itself. This new emphasis on finding and overcoming more sporting ways to the top also encouraged a new sense of self-reliance in the climbers.

Typical of the new wave was Albert Frederick Mummery, a myopic, stoop-shouldered tannery owner from London with a likeable personality and a forceful leading ability on Alpine rock and snow. Mummery began his Alpine climbing career traditionally enough, employing

Two of the **Chamonix Aiguilles** of the **Mont Blanc** Massif. On the left is **Aiguille des Grands Charmoz** (3,445m) and on the right, the **Aiguille du Grépon** (3,482m)

guides between 1879 and 1889 when he first displayed a talent for high-standard mountaineering, solving several of the outstanding Alpine problems of the day, such as the *Zmutt Ridge* of the Matterhorn and the Traverse of the **Aiguille du Grépon** (3,482m). Despite this, Mummery was effectively blackballed from the Alpine Club for murkily unclear reasons – there were rumours that he was a tradesman (owning a tannery apparently did not sit comfortably with the well-heeled Milords of the Alpine

Club) and his political philosophy was fairly radical (he co-authored a book on political economy). He may have been regarded as somewhat too left-leaning by the more snobby sections of the AC establishment.

Mummery's real influence on the direction of Alpine climbing really lay in his achievements after 1891 when he was not only allowed into the Alpine Club at last, but also started climbing without guides. Mummery's magnetic personality attracted a talented group of climbers about him, including Norman Collie, Geoffrey Hastings, Cecil Slingsby and Lily Bristow.

Most of his Alpine climbing partners had trained on Lakeland crags but curiously, Mummery did not care for English climbing. 'Climbing as practiced at Wasdale Head is both difficult and dangerous,' he said. This statement seems somewhat at odds with his Alpine exploits. In 1891 he almost pulled off the futuristic ascent of the *North Face* of the **Aiguille du Plan** (3,673m) a huge cascade of steep ice which was not climbed for a further 33 years. This epitomised Mummery's bold, modern style of alpine climbing, which may have had something to do with a physical deformity to his spine. It meant he could not carry heavy loads – he simply had to go fast and light. He was also intensely shortsighted – which probably accounted for his legendary hopelessness at route finding. This seems to have caused him to blunder into groundbreaking technical situations which he then had to climb his way out of. Between 1892 and 1893, Mummery also embarked on a long campaign of difficult rock routes, often accompanied by the female alpinist Lily Bristow, leading to his famous joke that

"All mountains appear doomed to pass through three stages: An inaccessible peak – The most difficult ascent in the Alps – An easy day for a lady."

This was merely an ironic tribute to the ability of the amazing Bristow who led many of the pitches of their climbs and who probably had more rock climbing experience than any other woman up to that point. Unfortunately their partnership was cut short after 1893, presumably thanks to the intervention of Mrs Mummery.

Mummery went on to lead the first guideless ascent of the steep, Italian side of Mont Blanc, on a climb which had only had five ascents by gifted climbers employing quality guides. It waited another 10 years for a repeat and illustrated how far ahead in the alpine climbing game were Mummery and his compatriots. Before Mummery left the scene in 1895, buried under an avalanche on faraway **Nanga Parbat** (8,125m), Mummery published his seminal book, *My Climbs in the Alps and Caucasus*. In it he laid out his central mountaineering philosophy.

"The essence of the sport lies, not in ascending a peak, but in struggling with and overcoming difficulties"

It was a sentiment which was readily taken up by continental climbers, but which still met resistance amongst some British mountaineers. It was nevertheless, an idea whose time had come and was the central tenet that would drive forward the next phase of climbing.

The **Alps**

The European Alps are the most famous mountains in the world and the scene of the first mountaineering adventures in the modern sense of the word. However, the word *alp* originally referred to the upland hill pastures which local herdsmen used as summer grazing. It was mistaken by the earliest visitors to refer to the entire mountain. The range, which stretches in an arc from the Mediterranean hinterland near Nice to the neighbourhood of Ljubljana in Slovenia and Vienna in Austria contains western Europe's highest mountain, **Mont Blanc** (4,807m) and over 50 other summits over 4,000m high. There are also hundreds of mountains between 3,500m and 4,000m in height. The range is thus heavily glaciated and many peaks are permanently snow-covered, although most glaciers have been in retreat for the last 150 years and the Alps are becoming more arid. The conditions encountered by modern alpinists are often very different from those tackled during the Golden Age of Alpine climbing in the mid-19th century, when more snow and ice occupied the slopes, ridges and summits. Another major difference is the proliferation of mountain huts and, in many areas, cable cars which make the approaches to the climbs logistically much less difficult than in the pioneers' day. Despite the globalisation of climbing as an activity, mountaineers the world over still look towards the Alps as a kind of spiritual home and return year after year to climb the classic routes or hunt for new approaches to summits.

A view of the Mer de Glace from the Leschaux Hut

On the Rock

(1880–1914)

Brag, sir, merely brag, that,

I have no doubt, is their enjoyment…

men struggling to degenerate into apes.

*Anonymous Wasdale tourist after
sharing hotel with climbers, 1890s*

Left: *Napes Needle*, **Great Gable**, Cumbria

The rise of the rock climber (1880–1914)

The slanting rays from a late afternoon sun were beginning to bronze the steep flanks of **Great Gable** (899m) as a lone figure, clad in nailed boots and stout tweed jacket, scrabbled his way up a striking pinnacle of rock. Pausing briefly on a ledge below the final steepening, he flung a series of small stones onto the top of the pinnacle. One of three stones stuck there, encouraging the climber to continue up the final twenty feet of the soaring needle, all the while 'feeling as small as a mouse climbing a milestone'. His hands finally grasped the flat edged top of the pinnacle and, with his heels sticking out over draughty nothingness, the climber made a couple of athletic movements to land on the summit. Walter Parry Haskett-Smith raised himself to his feet, panting slightly with the exertion and not a little exhilaration, and grinned from ear to ear as he took in the

expansive panorama of crag and fell stretching down to the distant sea beyond Wasdale. Then he began to wonder how he was going to get down again…

Haskett-Smith's solo climb of *Napes Needle* in June 1886 was only a small event in terms of physical magnitude (the route was only 70 feet long, and the *Needle* is merely an outlying rock pinnacle partly detached from the main mass of Great Gable's crags), but in philosophical terms it symbolised a fundamental sea-change in the relationship between climbers and mountains. By the 1880s climbers were becoming less fixated on the concept of 'the summit', and instead were turning more towards the notion of climbing for its own sake. People like Haskett-Smith had actively begun seeking out more difficult ways of ascending not only mountains, but also buttresses and cliffs or even, as in the case of *Napes Needle*, tiny bits of cliffs. Viewed from the context of the 21st century it seems difficult to comprehend just what a radical departure this was. However, it must be remembered that many mountaineers were still in thrall to the idea that climbing was part of the wider endeavour of scientific exploration, and that engaging in rock gymnastics on small outcrops purely for the pleasure of the exercise somehow demeaned the activity, de-intellectualising it and reducing it to the level of cheap stunts and showmanship. The stuffy attitude of some Alpine Club traditionalists emphasised the emerging split in mountaineering, dubbing the new wave of crag and outcrop climbers as

Owen Glynne Jones

'chimney-sweeps'. Even some of the practitioners of the new style of climbing sounded embarrassed about their activities; W.R. Lester actually apologised for 'a pure piece of mountaineering gymnastics' when reporting the ascent of what was arguably the first technical rock climb in Scotland, *The Black Shoot of Glas Maol*, in 1892.

But it wasn't only the attitudes towards what constituted climbing that were changing. Hand in glove with the evolving perspectives were social changes that were bringing a wider range of men (for it was still overwhelmingly a male-dominated activity) into the mountains. The mid-19th century Golden Age of alpinism had been largely driven by well-to-do upper-middle-class professionals or the leisured upper-class. The numbers engaging in the activity remained relatively small; they were, after all, the privileged few who possessed both the time and resources necessary to finance extended European holidays and employ guides. The evolution of a domestic climbing scene, however, opened up the activity to a much larger constituency, drawn from the burgeoning middle-classes. Typical of this new breed of enthusiastic, less-formal climber was an engineer from London who was to shake up the climbing community with a series of outstanding and innovative climbs: Owen Glynne Jones.

The first rock athlete
Owen Glynne Jones

O.G. Jones has been dubbed 'the first rock athlete', by virtue of his muscular, almost recklessly gymnastic style of climbing. However, he was far from universally admired; many of his fellow climbers thought him abrasive and boastful.

'He had studied his own physical powers as a chauffeur studies a car and for that reason he talked a great deal about himself', sneered Haskett-Smith. But there was more to Jones than just a loud mouth, a strong nerve and some very strong fingers. He was arguably the man who, more than any other, really expanded the limits of climbing, encouraging it to break free of its traditional shackles by his obsessive pursuit of hard, technical free-climbing as an end in itself, rather than simply training for real mountains. As if this concept wasn't radical enough, his approach to first ascents was also strikingly modern, as exemplified by his use of a top-rope to practice the crux of the very severe route, *Kern Knotts Crack*, prior to the first ascent in 1896. He also introduced an adjectival grading system for categorising the difficulty of climbs which still forms the basis of the British system to this day. However, on top of all this Jones possessed an historically precocious ability to promote his exceptional skill by the use of media contacts. He was one of the earliest climbers to be featured regularly and prominently in photographs, thanks to his association with the pioneers of adventure photography, the Abraham Brothers of Keswick. They forged a symbiotic relationship with Jones, he provided words, they provided the pictures. It was a winning combination, and their 1897 book, *Rock Climbing in the English Lake District*, fairly fizzes with Jones's exuberance. Although the exercise provoked further resentment amongst many of his peers (there was revulsion over the commercial exploitation of what many climbers considered their private pleasure) the book proved Jones to be more than simply a publicity seeking braggart, and amply demonstrated his credentials as a great communicator.

'A taste for companionable chaos'
Wasdale Head, base camp of British rock climbing (1890–1914)

Although Jones was one of the outstanding personalities of the early era of British rock climbing, he was but one of many talented characters beginning to populate the sport. The favoured meeting place for the early climbing community was the Wasdale Head Hotel at the head of Wast Water in the south-western Lake District. From here the cliffs below England's highest peaks could be easily reached and explored. Every Easter, Christmas and Whitsun between 1890 and the Great War, groups of like-minded fellows would escape the stifling social constraints of late-Victorian domestic and professional life and gather to form the world's first climbing scene. There were no rules, and an atmosphere of relaxed tolerance prevailed. 'In

...men struggling to degenerate into apes

The **Abraham** Brothers

George Dixon Abraham (1872–1965)

The Keswick-based Abraham Brothers were the first people to promote adventure sports in the media by virtue of their photo-reportage of the leading activists of the day. They managed to cart the monstrous plate-camera photographic apparatus of the late-Victorian period into areas only compact capsule 35mm would dare venture today. Always innovative, they also made one of the first climbing films, featuring an ascent of *Napes Needle*, in 1911.

The pair worked closely with the pre-eminent rock-gymnast of the day, O.G. Jones, and their working methods sound very familiar to anyone currently aspiring to shoot the cover photo of a modern climbing magazine. As Jones recounted: 'We composed our limbs to a photographic quiescence. Ashley had a splendid wide-angled lens. 'Mr Jones! I can't see you, your clothes are so dark, will you take off your coat?' There may have been no Fuji Velvia or bright red 'muscle vests' in the 1890s, but the Abrahams knew the importance of drawing attention to their main subject amidst a mass of dark crag. Their dedication paid off and resulted in the forerunner of all the lavishly illustrated 'coffee-table' climbing books. *Rock-Climbing in the English Lake District*, published 1897, was the result of collaboration with Jones. It broke new ground and was immediately hailed as a classic. Although Jones died in 1899, his book has always been in demand and the Abrahams went on to

Ashley Perry Abraham (1876–1951)

repeat their success with several others featuring Scotland, North Wales and the Alps although none quite reached the classic heights of *Rock-Climbing in the English Lake District* without Jones's subversive prose. The die was cast, however, and publishers have never looked back since.

These first forays into the commercial exploitation of rock climbing inevitably attracted criticism from sections of the climbing establishment, although the brothers were still liked by most due to their genial nature and the fact that they were very good climbers. Indeed the Abrahams made many significant rock-climbs, scattering first ascents around Scotland, the Lakes and Wales, and playing an important part in devising the first reliable belaying techniques. Nevertheless, their rôle as popularisers of the sport has had the most lasting significance. George's book *British Mountain Climbs*, for example, ran to six editions between 1908 and 1948 and was immensely influential in the development of British climbing, encouraging many people to take up the sport.

The brothers' legacy of action photographs of early climbing is also the finest record of this period in the world and continue to illustrate books and exhibitions to this day, including of course, the National Mountaineering Exhibition.

Ashley Abraham *(left)*, President of the Fell & Rock Club 1907–08 and George Abraham, Vice President, 1908–10

the evening', recorded G.T. Lowe in 1896, 'round the long dining table were gathered upwards of 30 men in strange costumes of rough tweed and as they ate with wondrous appetites, their talk was of rocks, hand-holds, traverses, arêtes, and all the peculiar jargon of the mountaineer's art.'

During earlier climbing meets in the 1880s, an air of scholarly decorum had characterised the gatherings. Following a strenuous day climbing mossy gullies, the hotel would be filled with the quiet talk of cultured gentlemen accompanied by clouds of pipe-smoke.

By contrast, a distinct air of boisterousness marked the 1890s. Although the 'smoke room' remained a safe haven for earnest discussion by veterans, elsewhere the younger men were less restrained in their behaviour. An anarchic club atmosphere developed, accompanied by by frankly non-academic chatter and rowdy behaviour centred on the billiard room. This was used as an impromptu gymnasium for athletic games, one of which involved clearing a corner of the table with both feet in a single vault. Another test was 'traversing the table': attempting to pass over and under the table without touching the floor. Inevitably the cloth became torn and remained so. The devastated table was used to play a new game: 'Billiard Fives' which was effectively mass participation table football using billiard balls. The barging of opponents was allowed and the balls frequently flew from the table, endangering players and spectators alike. (The amazingly tolerant landlord, Dan Tyson, merely put wire netting up to protect the windows.) The plaster on the walls became pockmarked by direct hits until the billiard room began to resemble a war zone.

'By Jove!' remarked a startled hotel guest observing the cheering ruck, as balls rebounded

Scafell Pinnacle

Scafell and
Napes Needle

The Lake District's Scafell massif contains the highest mountain in England – **Scafell Pike** (977m) – and one of the largest climbing cliffs in Britain on the neighbouring peak of **Scafell** (963m), itself the second highest English summit. The two Scafells are separated by a deep cleft called *Mickledore*, the traverse of which requires steep scrambling and a short section of moderate rock climbing called *Broad Stand*. It was during the descent of this feature in 1802 that the poet Coleridge experienced rock climbing for the first time and had what modern climbers refer to as an 'epic'. Scafell cliff was the scene of many of the early adventures undertaken by the pioneering Victorian cragsmen who lodged in the nearby Wasdale Head Hotel in the valley below.

Also accessible from the same hotel are the sunnier cliffs of **Great Gable** (899m), a slightly lower mountain to the west and also very popular with the pioneer climbers. At the base of the section of the cliffs known as the *Great Napes* lies a detached pinnacle of rock 18m high: *Napes Needle*. The solo ascent of this spectacular monolith by Haskett-Smith in 1886 is often taken to symbolise the birth of modern British rock climbing. Despite its diminutive stature, the *Needle* is such an icon of British climbing that it has attracted a disproportionate amount of attention. It now boasts eight independent ways of reaching its tiny summit, the most recent one pioneered in 1999 by Keswick climber Stephen Reid after a gap of 85 years!

John **Collie** (1859–1942)

John Norman Collie, a University College of London Professor of Organic Chemistry, was one of those astonishing late-Victorian polymaths who flourished during a brief period of British history when Empire at its height channelled some of its riches towards tenured scholarship. It allowed gentlemen of even relatively modest background, but high ability, to build brilliant academic careers, and still have a quarter of the year off to go exploring interesting undiscovered parts of the globe.

Collie helped pioneer climbing both in the Lake District (where he achieved the first Grade V winter climb in 1891) and the Cuillin of Skye. Together with local Gael John Mackenzie he climbed every peak in the range between 1888 and 1896, including the last unclimbed summit in Britain. His climbs in Glencoe and on Ben Nevis in 1894 are often taken as the beginning of serious mountaineering on the Scottish mainland.

In the Alps he was part of the 1890s British élite band of alpinists led by A.F. Mummery and was involved in several of the latter's ground-breaking guideless ascents.

As if all this was not enough, Collie helped initiate climbing exploration in the Lofoten Islands, the Himalaya and the Canadian Rockies, a range in which he was particularly energetic, making a clutch of first ascents and discovering the giant Columbia Icefield.

On top of all this he was tall, good looking and although he remained a bachelor all his life, he was a big hit with the opposite sex. An envious friend noted on a trip to Canada: 'The ladies spied him. Next moment his person reclined in a low chair, the centre of an admiring circle, while two fair dames, each supporting on high one of his neatly bandaged legs, tested with dainty fingers the sharpness of his Mummery screws.'

Collie had a reputation as an aesthete, wore sharp tweeds, smoked a Meerschaum pipe and was an expert on oriental art, wine,

food and cigars. When Collie went to Norway, 'crowds flocked to see him under the impression that he was Sherlock Holmes.' That he chipped the odd rock hold, believed in the Loch Ness Monster and claimed he was chased down **Ben Macdhui** (1,309m) by the ghostly 'Grey Man' did nothing to diminish the respect in which he was held by his peers.

As befits his enigmatic reputation, he retired to live alone on the Isle of Skye, taking rooms at the Sligachan Hotel within sight of his beloved Cuillin. Just before his death in 1942, he was observed by the young RAF pilot Richard Hillary on leave in Skye. 'We were alone in the inn, save for one old man who had returned there to die. His hair was white but his face and bearing were still those of a great mountaineer, though he must have been a great age. He never spoke, but appeared regularly at meals to take his place at a table, tight-pressed against the windows, alone with his wine and his memories. We thought him rather fine.'

dangerously off the walls, 'What a game! No wonder we couldn't play this afternoon, the ball must be covered in notches.'

The non-climbing guests remained utterly bemused by the eccentric behaviour of the climbers. Pioneer climber Lehman Oppenheimer recorded the opinion of one: 'Brag, sir, merely brag, that, I have no doubt, is their enjoyment… men struggling to degenerate into apes.'

But most of the climbers were far from becoming apes If O.G. Jones represented the athletic extreme of the new style of climber, Professor Norman Collie exemplified high intellectual extreme which still marked out the climbing scene. Collie's scientific achievements included helping in the discovery of neon and taking the first X-ray photograph for the purpose of medical examination. His polymathic genius extended to mountaineering too, where he excelled both on rock and ice and as a pioneer in the Greater Ranges.

With a range and richness of characters such as Jones and Collie involved, it is hardly surprising that the new sport of rock climbing advanced rapidly from basic beginnings to a high level of technical proficiency.

Climbs for all seasons

At the beginning of the 1880s climbers had mostly confined themselves to the illusory security of gully lines, where the blinkers of the sidewalls reduced the sense of exposure when climbing high off the ground. Haskett-Smith was one of the first to break out from the

The **evolution** of **climbing equipment**

1

The achievements of the pioneers are all the more impressive when one considers the rudimentary equipment available to them. Haskett-Smith and others had made their early climbs ropeless –

"We classed ropes with spikes and ladders, as a means by which bad climbers were enabled to go where none but the best climbers had any right to be".

They soon appreciated that a safety back-up was going to be necessary if they were to progress to more difficult climbs. The 'alpine rope' was introduced to the Lake District in 1885 but early attempts at deploying it were confused and risible: it might as well have not been there. Climbers moved tied together as though in the Alps, where speed was of the essence because the climbs were much longer. In Britain it merely meant that if one fell, most likely all would, as they did not anchor themselves to the rock. The rope's presence was thus largely psychological, although some climbers like Jones were more creative. He began threading ropes behind chockstones in cracks, along the principles followed by modern rock protection devices: a trick which saved him on more than one occasion. Early climbers were also often encumbered by a six-foot fell pole which they employed as a kind of British alpenstock. They used it as part walking stick, part vaulting-pole for leaping becks and rills. However, as the

climbs became more and more tricky, the pole became more of a nuisance (Haskett-Smith wasted considerable time fishing his out of a crack in which it had stuck prior to his groundbreaking climb of *Napes Needle*). It became replaced by the only slightly less cumbersome four-foot ice-axe. However the latter was essential in the often icy conditions of the day, and even in summer could be employed to good effect 'gardening' the earth, vegetation and loose blocks which choked many of the holds of the untrodden terrain which they hoped to climb. Clothing remained traditional. The hard-wearing Norfolk tweed jacket with its copious poachers' pockets useful for carrying sandwiches was standard attire, along with baggy knee breeches. On their feet, the nailed boot was essential, enabling them to bite through mud, moss and lichen and climb in all weathers. Only when it got really wet on very delicate ground did climbers take off their boots, and proceed in stockinged feet.

Whymper's hat and
Michel Croz's rosary beads

Whymper's ice-axe and goggles

One of Whymper's crampons –
or 'climbing irons' as they were called

One of Hadow's boots

gloomy defiles and on to open rock walls and slabs by the mid-1880s. Following this liberation, the degree of difficulty rapidly rose from climbs which were, in effect, little more than scrambles above big drops, to technical climbs, many of which are still regarded as respectably stiff challenges even today. Even more remarkable is the fact that many of the Lakeland climbs were completed under severe winter conditions. Winters were longer and more severe in the last decades of the nineteenth century than today and it was common for ice and snow to be present at the Christmas and Easter vacations favoured by the Wasdale climbers. Ambitious climbers, hungry for first ascents or early repeats, frequently ended up climbing under winter conditions whether they liked it or not. Norman Collie's ascent of *Steep Gill* on **Scafell** (963m) at Christmas 1891, for example, today ranks as a Grade V climb; the first of its level of difficulty ever achieved. Such a standard was not reached again for another four decades, and only became regularly achieved by the 1950s.

Postcards from the edge

Away from the hothouse of Wasdale Head, British climbing was developing in a more sedate fashion. In Scotland there were hundreds of mountains – but hardly any mountaineers. The formation of the Scottish Mountaineering Club in 1889 began to energise the latent Caledonian climbing community but even so, the early developments on the mountains of **Ben Nevis** (1,343m), Glencoe and Skye were mostly the work of visiting English climbers. In Wales, technical climbing was more advanced, again thanks mainly to the raiding Wasdale-trained

climbers, but also partly due to the efforts of locally-based Welshman J.M. Archer Thomson. He had begun climbing in 1894 at a time when only twelve climbs had been recorded in the whole of Snowdonia. Within two years he had added a further fourteen and became highly influential in leading Welsh climbing away from the murky gullies and onto the open slabs and faces.

In other regions the first climbing probes were also beginning to be made; Aleister Crowley and A.F. Mummery had tackled the dangerous chalk cliffs of Beachy Head, while A.W. Andrews was starting his life-long, but usually solitary love affair with Cornish sea cliffs. However, perhaps most significantly of all for future developments, the millstone grit outcrops around Sheffield and in the Peak District were beginning to be explored by J.W. Puttrell. Although small, the climbs here were technically fierce and required an extremely high standard of ability. Puttrell and his successors were to hone their techniques and then re-import them to the home of rock climbing, the mountains around Wasdale, where standards would be raised to spectacular new heights by the eve of the Great War.

The end of the beginning

Despite the rudimentary safety measures employed by the pioneers, it is a testament to their skill and judgement that until 1903 there had been no serious climbing accidents on British crags. All this changed on a blustery day in September of that year when a party of four climbers fell to their death from Scafell Crag. The inadequate belaying technique of the time

had allowed all four to be pulled off after the leader slipped, and it remained the worst single British climbing accident for over half a century. The accident had a traumatising effect on the Lakeland climbing scene and the Wasdale Head community seemed to lose its momentum. Instead, the hub of innovative rock climbing passed to Snowdonia, where the brilliant alpinist Geoffrey Winthrop Young began organising regular parties in order to begin a networking system of talented climbers. Nevertheless, after a few years, standards began to rise once more and reached a breakthrough in 1914 when the brilliant gritstone-trained climber Siegfried Herford visited the Lake District and climbed a direct line up the imposing *Central Buttress* of Scafell. The climb, which was the first to be given the climbing grade of 'Hard Very Severe', was far in advance of anything attempted hitherto and was a real leap into the future. A new era of mountaineering appeared to be about to commence, but before it could do so, it was snuffed out by an eruption of machine guns and artillery on the Continent.

Left: Siegfried Herford astride the *Great Flake*, *Central Buttress*, **Scafell**

His death in the Great War, along with many other great talents, signified the end of an era in British climbing

At 5,642m, **Elbrus** is the highest peak in Europe

The Great Game

Exploring the mountains of the Caucasus, the Americas and the Greater Ranges of Asia

(1870–1910)

Personally, I believe that, supposing the actual natural difficulties to be overcome, the air, or want of it, will prove no obstacle to the ascent of the very highest peaks in the world.

William Woodman Graham, pioneer Himalayan climber, 1880s

Just as the Golden Age of Alpine peak-bagging was coming to an end, a nearby range of even bigger mountains became available to the collector of pristine summits. The Russian army had been struggling to subdue the country's border states for some time but in 1864 it finally gained control of the security situation in the areas containing the Caucasus. The campaign had also involved the mapping and survey of the area in some detail and this enabled British mountaineers to plan an extension of their own mountaineering assaults into this area.

Caucasus feeding frenzy
(1870–1890)

The Caucasus were on average around 1,000m higher than most of the Alps and contained the highest mountain in Europe, **Elbrus** (5,642m). They were a mouth-watering prospect for Golden Age stalwarts such as Adolphus Moore and Douglas Freshfield who were quick to take advantage of the new opportunities. By 1868 Elbrus had been climbed but further exploration was stalled temporarily as local wars reignited. By the 1880s the British were back in force with A.F. Mummery leading the charge and climbing many 5,000m+ peaks. A less famous, but equally impressive British pioneer of the period was the Liverpool barrister John Cockin. In 1888 he bagged several arduous and technical 5,000m peaks in a busy three-week spell.

In other areas of Europe, intrepid British pioneers were also opening up the mountains to the sound of ringing ice-axes and the crunch of nailed boots. Cecil Slingsby, a wealthy squire and textile manufacturer from Yorkshire, began the exploration of the Norwegian Jotunheimen and made many fine ascents.

When his reputation as a climber came under fire from some jealous local mountaineers he took a local girl 'dressed in her Sunday best' to the top of a mountain by a route which his rivals claimed was the hardest climb in Norway.

'We reached the summit, raised a loud cheer, and put Marie on the top of the little cairn, and very bonny she looked in her picturesque costume.'

He also added that they hadn't bothered with a rope – that shut his detractors up.

New mountains in a New World
(1870–1911)

The completion of the Canadian Pacific Railway in 1885 opened up a whole new world of peaks to British climbers without the inconvenience associated with foreign languages. There were plenty of other problems though: the mountains' bush-bound inaccessibility, mosquitoes and rotten limestone rock. Although US climbers were the first to recognise the climbing possibilities, probing the Selkirk Range to the west, it was not long before British climbers arrived. In 1897 they were joined by a huge fan

Mount Assiniboine (3,610m) also known as 'The Matterhorn of the Rockies'

Sir Martin Conway

Edward Whymper

of the Canadian Rockies, Norman Collie, who eventually made six trips there between 1897 and 1911, discovering the Columbia Icefield, the greatest ice-bound area in the Rockies and made many significant first ascents. A vigorous competition for prized summits later developed between Collie and James Outram, an expatriate Briton who pipped Collie to the first ascent of the 'the Matterhorn of the Rockies', the spectacular **Mount Assiniboine** (3,610m). The old Tiger of the Alps, Edward Whymper, also entered the arena in 1901 as a guest of the Canadian Pacific Railway who hoped to use his fame to promote the area as a tourist destination. Collie was horrified at the thought of yet more competition in a massive region he had hoped to keep to himself.

"All I can say is damn the man!
Why I am so mad about it is that it is not
done for sport at all or because Whymper
has any real liking for the hills.
From the beginning it is dollars…"

He need not have worried. Whymper was by now a mere shadow of his former driven self and was quite content to potter about on small mountains near the railway. Whymper's final burst of exploratory mountaineering energy had been expended 22 years earlier in the same hemisphere, but further south.

South of the border

Modern exploratory mountaineering had begun in earnest almost a decade and half earlier in South America, thanks to the tireless search for new conquests by Edward Whymper. Whymper had more or less retreated from the European Alpine arena after the trauma of his Matterhorn adventure. However, the celebrity status he had acquired in the course of his climbing drove him onwards to further exploratory efforts.

He visited Greenland in 1867 and 1874, perhaps seeking to fulfil his boyhood ambitions to become a polar hero, but had not managed to achieve any geographical feat of significance. Turning once more to mountains, he cast his eyes across the Atlantic to the little-known Andes. The political turmoil of the South American continent forced him to focus his efforts on the comparative tranquillity of Ecuador and he embarked on a campaign of peak-bagging there in 1879. Accompanying him was his old Matterhorn rival Carrel, now reconciled.

After several abortive attempts they eventually climbed **Chimborazo** (6,267m) previously thought to be the highest mountain in the world, but during the course of the ascent suffered both frostbite and, to Whymper's discomfit, altitude sickness. On the much lower peaks of the Alps he had not known such a problem and the revelation that he acclimatised poorly greatly distressed him. Nevertheless, with characteristic tenacity, Whymper persisted and, in a campaign reminiscent of his great Alpine campaign of 1864/5, he swept through a slew of unclimbed Ecuadoran peaks. Although none of

these mountains was technically difficult by modern standards, the significance of Whymper's efforts in the Andes was that it showed that by dint of careful planning and management of resources, British climbers could mount successful mountaineering campaigns in the most distant foreign ranges. His book about his travels, published eleven years later, would be used as a blueprint for other exploratory ventures, such as those by Sir Martin Conway, an urbane art historian and unabashed mountain Romantic.

Conway had begun his exploration of non-European ranges by mounting a huge expedition to the Karakoram, but by 1898 he was following in the footsteps of Whymper to the Andes. **Aconcagua** (6,959m) in Argentina, the highest mountain in South America, was the great prize, but they warmed up first on smaller 6,000m+ peaks of the Bolivian Cordillera Real, unaware that the indigenous Indians were seriously considering killing them for profaning the summits of their sacred peaks with their presence.

The eventual assault on Aconcagua failed just below the top, and Conway lost interest in South America, and climbing in general. Perhaps all that planning and amateur bureaucracy had killed the romance for him: 'Mountains had called me as things of beauty and wonder, things terrible and sublime, and instead of glorying in their splendour, here I was spending months in outlining the vagrant plan of them on a piece of paper. That realisation ended my mountain career.'

The **Caucasus**

The Caucasus form a geographical boundary between Europe and Asia. The range stretches nearly 1,000km from the Caspian Sea to the Black Sea and contains the highest mountain in Europe: Elbrus (5,642m). The mountains are on average around 1,000m higher than those in the Alps although the range lies three degrees of latitude further south which means that, although the mountains are snow-capped and glaciated, the snow-line is higher and the ice-fields smaller. The area has always been geo-politically sensitive, a factor which has periodically stymied its mountaineering exploration ever since the days of the early alpine pioneers who moved into the area following the Golden Age later in the 19th Century. British teams pioneered much of the early climbing, but visits to the range by western climbers were sporadic during the era of the Soviet Union, when most climbing was undertaken by Russians. Since the end of the Cold War access has become easier in places, although the fact that the mountains straddle parts of several volatile former Soviet republics such as Chechnya and Georgia, means that many areas remain effectively out of bounds.

Right: Via Tak (3,900m) in the Caucasus

The road to K2

(1882–1893)

The Duke of the Abruzzi

In 1892 Sir Martin Conway mounted a large expedition to the mighty Hispar and Biafo Glacier systems of the Karakoram.

The area had been under the suzerainty of local warlords through much of the nineteenth century but a campaign by the British Indian Army to bring the region under a client-state relationship with The Raj had proved successful and allowed scientific expeditions to visit the region. Conway thought it ideal for a joint scientific/climbing venture and took with him the great Swiss guide Mattias Zurbriggen, climber Oscar Eckenstein and Gurkha officer Charles Bruce and some of his men. The trip was riven with dissension due to personality clashes between the High Tory Conway and the social radical Eckenstein, plus squabbles over finances with Bruce. Nevertheless they mapped the glaciers, the biggest outside the polar regions and moved on to the great Baltoro Glacier which led on to a further glacier stretching to the foot of the world's second highest peak, K2 (8,611m). Their climbing achievements, although they were modest, reached heights of over 6,700m.

The expedition was influential in that it set a trend for large-scale expeditions in the area, and was the first probe in reconnoitring the mighty K2. It was followed up in 1902 by the first attempt on the mountain itself by Eckenstein in company with a team including the outrageous Aleister Crowley, the self-styled 'Great Beast 666'. Crowley, a diabolist and early proponent of free love and the recreational use of drugs, was quite a handy climber and it was probably this combination of climbing skill and unorthodox personality which attracted him to Eckenstein, who was regarded with a degree of suspicion by the Alpine Club establishment as much for his being half-German as for his left-leaning political outlook. This may have partly explained how Eckenstein came to be arrested as a spy when he entered India, only avoiding being deported after a personal interview with the Viceroy. Despite these and other difficulties, the expedition, eventually reached a high point of 6,532m. Crowley returned to the Himalaya three years later when he caused more consternation on **Kangchenjunga** (8,586m) by refusing to help after an accident which killed three porters. The attempt fizzled out shortly afterwards in characteristically acrimonious fashion and remained a farcical footnote in the history of the mountain.

Hardly surprisingly, such antics did not impress the climbing world. Instead it was Conway's heavyweight trip which was the inspiration for a follow up on an even more lavish scale by the Italian Duke of the Abruzzi who made an attempt on K2 accompanied by 11 compatriots, and 6 tonnes of luggage carried by over 500 porters. It was an expedition drawn-up on a military scale and, although they made a spirited attempt on the mountain, it was too difficult and ambitious a mountain for a team constrained by Edwardian technology. The scale of the expedition, however, **was** to be highly influential in shaping future developments in climbing in the Greater Ranges.

The lightweight alternative

Although Conway's excursions into the high Asian mountains were spectacular, they were not the first British mountaineering ventures in the region. The initial climbing in the Greater Ranges of Asia had been a much more low-key affair. The enigmatic barrister William Woodman Graham was the first to visit the area purely for climbing purposes. He had no interest at all in scientific exploration and travelled to the Indian Garhwal Himalaya in 1883 with a Swiss guide. He trekked around **Kangchenjunga** (8,586m) during the spring but was forced to retreat due to extreme cold and thanks to one of the porters accidentally burning his climbing boots. He returned to the Garhwal in the summer, freshly shod and with a change of guide, to explore the ranges surrounding the famously inaccessible Nanda Devi Sanctuary. They made an almost successful attempt on **Dunagiri** (7,066m) but were turned back by bad weather. The experience convinced Graham that he had nothing to fear from the rarefied atmosphere of these highest of mountains:

"The air, or want of it, will prove no obstacle to the ascent of the very highest peaks,"

was his prescient view. Graham made an attempt to penetrate the Nanda Devi Sanctuary by means of the difficult Rishi Ganga Gorge but was turned back by illness amongst his porters and the enormous scale of the gorge. It would not be traversed for another half century. Graham next climbed a very high mountain. That much appears to be certain. What it actually was is still a matter of contention. It could be, although it is unlikely, that it was **Changabang**

(6,866m), a peak only officially ascended for the first time in 1974. However, most authorities suspect Graham may have climbed a lower, 5,791m peak in the area, which was poorly mapped at the time, confusing the later reporting of his activities. He went on to climb another big mountain which he claimed was **Kabru** (7,316m). If so, this would have made it the highest mountain then climbed in the world. The debate over which peak he summited continues to this day – as does the mysterious Graham's fate, for he disappears from climbing history's radar after his momentous undertakings in the Himalaya. For many years it was claimed that he had lost all his money and emigrated to the US to become a cowboy. Satisfyingly romantic as this ending is, he had actually become the British Vice-Consul in an obscure Mexican town. Graham had apparently made enemies in the Alpine Club (his application for membership was resoundingly thrown out by an overwhelming majority of votes) and there appears to have been a deliberate rubbishing campaign against his reputation which has further muddied the facts of his achievements.

Whatever the actual details of the summits that Graham climbed, his achievements were well ahead of their time, adopting as they did a small-scale lightweight approach to climbing remote Himalayan peaks without bottled oxygen. Much the same, in fact, as though he were climbing in the Alps. His example was followed by several Edwardian pioneers such as the well-travelled Tom Longstaff who would follow in Graham's footsteps to the Garhwal before the Great War, attempting peaks around the Nanda Devi Sanctuary and embarking on 'a walk of some thousand miles [1,600km] across and around the Himalaya' to forbidden Tibet.

Aleister **Crowley** (1875–1947)

Crowley is one of the more memorable characters of British mountaineering history – for all the wrong reasons. Hopelessly addicted to self-publicity and opiates, he also dabbled in the occult, styling himself the 'Great Beast 666'.

As well as his fondness for sacrificing cats and goats, his notoriety soared when he set up a bohemian hippy-style commune in Sicily which advocated 1960s-style free love. The only problem was that this was in the 1920s. The popular press had a field day, dubbing him 'The Wickedest Man in the World'. He had difficulty getting overdraft facilities in later life.

In pure mountaineering terms, Crowley is significant as one of the pioneers of Himalayan climbing, being a member of the first expeditions to attempt the second and third highest peaks in the world, **K2** (8,611m) and **Kangchenjunga** (8,586m).

These expeditions were, predictably, a bit of a disaster. At one point on K2 Crowley chased off a team member at gunpoint after an argument, and when an avalanche killed three porters and injured two climbers on Kangchenjunga, Crowley famously remained sipping tea in his sleeping bag, despite the audibility of their cries. 'Not that I was over-anxious in the circumstances to render help. A mountain "accident" of this sort is one of things for which I have no sympathy whatever.'

Nevertheless, Crowley was clearly a handy climber. He was one of the Wasdale Head regulars during its heyday (making a new route up *Napes Needle*) and pioneered climbing on the chalk cliffs of Beachy Head. He was also one of the first to explore Mexican volcanoes, climbing **Popocatépetl** (5,452m) in 1900.

William Woodman Graham

Right: The view into Nepal as it might have been seen by W.W. Graham during his travels

At one point Graham glimpsed a view from a high ridge into equally mysterious Nepal:

"We were like Cortez seeing the Pacific for the first time; I was more elated by this enormous vista of the unknown than by any other discovery or ascent that I have ever accomplished."

Others were also active. Ex-Alpine Club President, Douglas Freshfield, turned from exploring the Caucasus in 1899 to circumnavigate the Kangchenjunga massif and reconnoitre approaches to the mountain. And a development of great significance occurred after 1907 when the innovative Scottish scientist, Alexander Kellas, began employing the local Himalayan

tribe, the Sherpas, in preference to the traditional Swiss guides. He used them extensively on his campaign of peak-bagging in the Kangchenjunga region, knocking off several outlying peaks, including the fourth highest climbed to that date, **Pauhunri** (7,128m). Also active in the Himalaya in the pre-war period was that other great alpine innovator, A.F. Mummery, who

General C.G. Bruce

finally got around to visiting the Greater Ranges in 1895.

Mummery's party was small but strong. It included two of the top climbers of the day, Norman Collie and Geoffrey Hastings, plus one of the most experienced Himalayan travellers, Charles Bruce with two of his Gurkhas, Raghobir and Goman Singh. They chose the isolated peak of **Nanga Parbat** (8,125m), the westernmost of the 8,000m Himalayan peaks situated on the Indus watershed, because it was not only big, but relatively close to accessible British territory and thus less expensive to visit than many big mountains. Mummery appears to have underestimated the scale of the mountain before him, writing optimistic letters home to his wife encouraged by the superficial lack of technical obstacles he perceived on the daunting *Diamir Face* of the

Himalayan giant. 'I don't think there will be any serious mountaineering difficulties on Nanga,' he wrote, 'I fancy the ascent will be mainly a question of endurance.' It was – but it was more endurance than they possessed. Mummery, Hastings and Collie together attempted some outlying peaks as training – but failed to get up them. They put their failure down to lack of training and altitude but in reality it was the difficulty of judging the new, bigger scale of everything compared with the Alps. After expending huge amounts of time and energy just moving around the foot of the huge mountain and undertaking some of the most technical rock climbing then achieved in the Himalaya, most of the party, apart from Mummery, was running out of steam and patience. While the others rested, Mummery set out to cross a pass to reconnoitre an unknown face of the massif with the two porters and disappeared – probably victims of an avalanche.

When later expeditions were mounted to the giant peaks of Asia, Mummery's lightweight approach with its unfortunate deaths were compared with the Duke of the Abruzzi's monster juggernaut to the very different mountain of K2, which had suffered no such casualties. Although both expeditions had failed to climb their respective objectives, the glib conclusion drawn from this tiny sample was that big peaks required big expeditions. A pattern had been set for the next phase of world mountaineering.

Dr Alexander Kellas (1868–1921)

Kellas, an absent-minded-looking chemistry lecturer at Middlesex Hospital was one of the first people to study the effects of altitude on humans. Accordingly, he was involved in the Everest Reconnaissance of 1921. The sight of his stooped dishevelled frame, his characteristic pebble glasses perched atop his pinched face caused George Mallory to say of him that he was: 'beyond description Scotch and uncouth in his speech – altogether uncouth,' although this very uncouthness delighted him. Mallory was in a minority however, others thought Kellas more couthy than uncouth. 'Although he was keenly interested in chemistry, he was even more interested in mountains',

said fellow chemist Norman Collie. The veracity of this assessment is proved by Kellas's climbing record which combined the Professor's interests in climbing and science.

Between 1907 and 1921 he made several visits to the Kangchenjunga region where he dispensed with usual imported European guides in favour of employing the mountaineering skills of indigenous hill people. 'They seemed more at home in the diminished pressure', reasoned the scientific Kellas.

One Nepalese tribe in particular, the Sherpas, he found to be especially reliable, and with these native guides he climbed several major peaks, including one of highest achieved at that time, **Pauhunri** (7,128m) in 1911.

Kellas's far-sighted collaboration with the Sherpas was not appreciated by everyone, especially stuffy traditionalists. Instead of applauding his innovative approach, the President of the Alpine Club sneered with a statement dripping with imperialist prejudice: 'Kellas has never climbed a mountain, but has only walked about on steep snow with a lot of coolies'. History, however, was to prove Kellas right not only on his prescient choice of local mountaineering support, but also in his advocacy of the use of bottled oxygen, although he always held that Everest 'could be ascended by a man of excellent physical and mental constitution in first-rate training, without adventitious aids…'.

Discovering Everest

5

Mount Everest (8,850m)

A ccording to popular legend, one momentous day in 1852 Radhanath Sikhdar, head of the Computing Office of the Grand Trigonometrical Survey of India, nervously knocked on the door of the Calcutta office of Sir Andrew Waugh, Surveyor General of India.

'What is it?' demanded Waugh of his quaking underling.

Sikhdar spluttered…

'I believe, sir, that I have found the highest mountain in the world'

Peak XV and the reluctant George Everest
(1850–1865)

Sikhdar, an arithmetical wizard, was the Grand Survey's computer whose it job was to evaluate and correlate all the surveyor's readings. Tucked away amongst the mass of data he had become startled by some amazing readings taken by John Armstrong in November 1847. Armstrong had observed a large, gleaming pyramidal peak shimmering in the sub-continental heat over 160km away. Despite the distance of the observation, the sheer size and bulk of the peak, designated simply, 'b', would have drawn the surveyor's gaze towards it magnetically as he continued taking his measurements, shielding his eyes from the glare of the sun as he jotted figures in his notebook. But it would take another five years before Sikhdar's painstaking analysis of all the surveying data would reveal that the mountain, now coded 'Peak XV', appeared to be over 8,840m high. Thus began a hundred-year obsession with the mountain by the British which has since spread to virtually every country on the planet.

Although Sikhdar's results were soon accepted, it was not the Indian surveyor who was honoured by lending his own name to the peak. Instead, in the authoritarian tradition of the British Empire's establishment, it was the Grand Trigonometrical Survey's erstwhile boss, Colonel George Everest. Ironically, Everest, who had commanded the Survey during its expansionist phase further south in the sub-continent prior to Peak XV's discovery, had never actually seen the mountain. Furthermore, he was positively embarrassed by the accolade and would have much preferred that indigenous nomenclature be retained for the peak. His protests were to no avail. Instead the imperial prerogatives of the day ignored the fact that the mountain already possessed a perfectly good local name; the Tibetan *Chomolungma*, (*Goddess Mother of the World*). Despite the passage of time and the lessening of such Anglo-centric attitudes, it is still as **Mount Everest** that the world's highest mountain is known by most people.

Pundits and Peaks
(1865–1900)

Once discovered, it was only a matter of time before thoughts turned towards mapping, exploring and climbing the mountain. In the mid-nineteenth century, however, the technical mountaineering skills and equipment required to tackle such a monster were in their infancy and realistic proposals to climb the mountain would have to wait until the sport began to mature around the turn of the century. In addition, it was not actually until the 1880s that it was thought possible for humans to survive above 6,700m. Until then many assumed, as did Asian adventurer Francis Younghusband, that 'The highest peak in the Himalaya must forever lie outside the range of human capacity'. But it was not just the mountaineering challenge that was formidable. Everest lay in one of the most inaccessible and remote places on the planet. Indeed, for 70 years after its discovery, no other surveyors managed to get within 160km of the peak, for the mountain lay in politically difficult terrain, being bounded to the south by the xenophobic Kingdom of Nepal and to the north by the equally insular Buddhist country of Tibet.

Despite these problems, covert surveillance continued to be undertaken in the Himalaya by the British throughout the nineteenth century. This was the era of the 'Great Game', the tactical jousting on the borders between the great

Sir Francis Younghusband

Captain Noel in Tibetan dress. He went on to become the expedition photographer on the 1922 and 1924 expeditions to Everest

empires of Imperial Britain and Tsarist Russia. Indigenous people were trained as masters of disguise in order to blend in with the local population while secretly spying out the country and its infrastructure.

These were the famous 'Pundits', a corruption of the Indian word *Pandit*, meaning 'educated man'. The first and most famously successful of these educated spies, Nain Singh, was in fact a native of the Himalaya. Nain and his cousins began infiltrating Nepal and Tibet from 1865 onwards, disguised variously as Punjabi horse dealers or Ladakhi traders. They had been trained to pace exactly 2,000 strides to a mile, enabling them to undertake elementary mapping and to memorise observations by constantly repeating them in a chant, pretending that this was a form of religious ritual so as not to arouse suspicion.

Singh was extremely successful, spending 21 months recording strategic terrain in Tibet and eventually entering the forbidden capital of Lhasa. Following several successful missions, he was awarded the Royal Geographical Society's Gold Medal for being an explorer who 'has added a greater amount of positive knowledge to the map of Asia than any individual of our time'.

The following two decades saw the expansion of the Pundit network, and despite the best efforts of Nepalis and Tibetans to keep their mountains and valleys secret, the British authorities began to acquire a detailed knowledge of the rugged

northern frontiers of the Raj. Although Nepal managed to stay aloof and closed to foreigners, Tibet was eventually bullied into grudging co-operation with the British in 1903 when British forces, commanded by Francis Younghusband, undertook an armed mission to Lhasa.

Trouble with Tibet (1903–4)

Younghusband, a hawkish commander in the British Indian Army, had already distinguished himself as a fanatically stoical explorer having crossed the Gobi Desert and Mustagh Pass, as well as exploring the Karakoram and Pamir mountain ranges. In a similar spirit he proposed an attempt to climb Everest in 1893, but soldiering duties on the volatile North-West Frontier ensured that his plans were constantly stymied. The Viceroy of India, Lord Curzon was also enthused by the idea, but for strategic and political reasons rather than adventurous ones. He went as far as making a formal request to the Nepalese for a British expedition to Everest, but was distracted from the enterprise by events relating to his belief that Tibet was threatened by Russian Imperial expansionism – a concern which was to lead to Younghusband's mission to Lhasa.

Younghusband easily fought his way to Lhasa; the small Tibetan army, armed with muskets, sling shots and leather cannons were no match for sepoys armed with Maxim machine-guns and 10-pounder artillery. When he reached Lhasa, he demanded that the Tibetans sign a treaty acquiescing to British demands. Because of the 'special relationship' thus forced by the British on the Tibetans, all

early expeditions to Everest would attempt the more difficult northern side, accessible through that country, rather than the less-technical – but closed – Nepalese side.

The mountain beckons (1905–1913)

As a result of the changed political circumstances, the way was open for the first attempt to climb the mountain. Curzon suggested to the President of the Royal Geographical Society that a joint expedition with the Alpine Club might be mounted. Surprisingly, the RGS was reluctant and there was some difficulty raising the money.

The scheme was saved in 1907 by Arnold Mumm, a wealthy climber and member of the Alpine Club, who generously offered to underwrite the expedition to mark the Club's 50th anniversary. But it was not to be. Curzon was forced to resign his Viceroyship due to a change of government and although his successor, Lord Minto, who was also a member of the Alpine Club, was supportive, the new Liberal British Secretary of State for India, John Morley, vetoed the venture.

Morley disavowed his predecessor's policies, and particularly abhorred the military intervention in Tibet instigated by Curzon. As a result he associated any scheme of the previous administration – even a climbing expedition – as a potential threat to the Anglo-Russian relations, which he was determined to improve. This emphatically put paid to the first attempt at an Everest expedition. Mumm's team went out to Asia anyway, but to the less politically sensitive area of the Indian Garhwal.

The **third** pole (1921–1922)

The Great War not only put paid to any further Everest exploration, it also took its grisly toll of experienced British mountaineers. Nevertheless, not long after the cessation of hostilities, the RGS and Alpine Club began the process of reviving interest in the project. Although professing scientific motives for climbing Everest, a major attraction for these bodies undoubtedly lay in salvaging national pride by achieving a achievement of geographical exploration to match recent feats in the polar regions. 'Now that the poles have been reached,' announced John Noel at a talk at the Royal Geographical Society in 1919, 'it is generally felt that the next and equally important task is the exploration and mapping of Mount Everest'. There was a feeling that Britain had been narrowly beaten in the race to claim these geographical prizes by foreigners and a determination that Everest should not be snatched from the country's grasp in the same way. In the eyes of the British, Everest had become 'The Third Pole'.

Once again the RGS and AC formed a joint committee to collaborate on the venture, but tensions developed early on, thanks to the different ambitions of the two organisations. The geographers were rather keener on careful survey and cartography than the climbers, who naturally were more concerned with bagging the peak as quickly as possible. Nevertheless, a compromise was reached which put ascent of the highest mountain in the world as the primary objective, but not at the expense of scientific exploration, which would be given a lot of weight in the planning. Even so, these split priorities, further exaggerated by personality clashes, would later cause problems when the first expedition actually left British shores.

Before all that however, there was the small matter of funding to be raised. A joint committee set to work with enthusiasm. Key players in moving the project forward included the familiar Francis Younghusband, General Charles Bruce, Charles Howard-Bury and President of the Alpine Club, Percy Farrar.

The joint Mount Everest Committee appointed a secretary, Arthur Hinks, a non-climbing RGS member whose boorish and cantankerous personality would dominate all Everest proceedings and irritate expedition members for the next 20 years. Even worse, given that they were ventures that relied heavily on private donations for support, Hinks had an almost pathological disdain for publicity. Given these disadvantages, it is remarkable that early Everest attempts got off the ground at all.

The chaos extended to the selection of the expedition team as well. Howard-Bury, who had already spent six months and a considerable amount of his own private fortune smoothing

Members of the 1921 Everest Expedition – *standing, from left:* Dr A.F.R. Wollaston, Lt. Col. C.K. Howard-Bury, Rand Heron, Harold Raeburn; *seated, from left:* George Mallory, Maj. E.O. Wheeler, G.H. Bullock, Maj. H.T. Morshead

the way on diplomatic visits to Tibet, was appointed overall leader of the expedition. The fifty-six-year old Scottish climbing veteran, Harold Raeburn was appointed 'Climbing Leader'. When it came to selecting lead climbers, the choice had been seriously restricted thanks to the toll of the Great War. One who had survived the carnage was a man who was destined to become the most famous mountaineer in the world: George Mallory.

Mallory was a master at Charterhouse public school and had long been the darling of the climbing establishment. Senior figures like Geoffrey Winthrop Young admired him on account of his striking good looks, aesthetic sensibilities and climbing ability. On top of all that, he had

Arthur Hinks

George **Mallory**
(1886–1924)

George Herbert Leigh Mallory and Mount Everest became almost inseparable in the public imagination during the first attempts to climb the mountain in the early 1920s. Both man and mountain became icons; the latter as a symbol of the terrible might of nature, and the former as the romanticised full-blooded Englishman rising to the challenge of overcoming its difficulties, giving his all before dying a glorious death.

Not for nothing did Geoffrey Winthrop Young dub him 'Sir Galahad'. The reality, though no less honourable, was rather more prosaic.

Mallory was introduced to Alpine climbing by one of his masters at Winchester School, Graham Irving. He displayed an aptitude for climbing, his natural athleticism compensating for a sometimes cavalier approach and a chronic absent-mindedness. His carelessness was legendary: climbing the **Finsteraarhorn** (4,274m) in Switzerland in 1909, for instance, Mallory forgot to tie onto the climbing rope and only became aware of the fact when he was in a very exposed position with a thousand-foot fall threatening. Such was his coolness, that he was able to maintain his composure and was able to re-attach himself.

This forgetfulness never left him; General Bruce, leader of the 1922 and 1924 Everest expeditions remarked that 'He is a great dear, but forgets his boots on all occasions'. Mallory went up to Cambridge in 1905 where he moved in exalted circles. Here he continued to hone his climbing skills and became well-known amongst influential members of the Alpine Club.

After the Great War, during which he served in several artillery units, he was one of the fortunate few to survive without serious injury. Thanks to his climbing and social credentials Mallory was an automatic choice as lead climber for the post-war Everest expeditions. By this stage Mallory was married, had children and was teaching at Charterhouse, but his friend Winthrop Young persuaded him that his future could be even more secure as a writer if he achieved the celebrity status assured by being the first to climb the world's highest peak.

In between expeditions, Mallory gave lectures in Britain and North America and it was during the US tour in 1923 that in response to the question:

'Why climb Everest?'

he is *alleged* to have made his famous reply:

'...because it's there!'

It seems unlikely that Mallory ever actually uttered the phrase; instead there is strong circumstantial evidence that it was a form of pithy journalistic shorthand invented by a reporter or sub-editor at the *New York Times*.

The disappearance of Mallory and Irvine on Everest in 1924 resulted in one of the longest-running mountaineering mysteries of all time, and the question of whether the duo may have summited has continued to excite the passions of historians ever since. The sensational discovery of Mallory's body by an American research expedition in 1999 resulted in an explosion of publicity and merely reinforced Mallory's position as the best known mountaineer in the world. It also served to re-ignite the debate as to whether he succeeded in reaching the top, but failed to provide conclusive answers one way or the other.

an impeccable social background, being stoutly middle-class (son of a clergyman) and highly cultured. Accompanying Mallory as a lead climber would be Guy Bullock. The team also included high-altitude physiologist Alexander Kellas, climbing medic Dr Wollaston and a couple of mountain surveyors Morshead and E.O. Wheeler.

When the expedition finally set sail, they must have presented anything but a united and professional appearance. Although the climbers had been grudgingly awarded a small grant of £50 each towards their equipment and clothing (raised to £100 'if necessary') by the abstemious Hinks, the choice of apparel had been left to individual climbers.

As a result a decidedly eclectic mixture of styles characterised the team. There were ancient tweeds and greatcoats, scarves and woolly cardigans, gabardine macs and leather motorcycling helmets, and socks knitted by wives and girlfriends. Today, it seems more like gear suitable for a group of schoolboys being sent off for a winter at a particularly draughty Scottish boarding school than the first attempt to climb the world's highest mountain. Most impressively sartorial of all was the team leader (and Irish squire) Howard-Bury, who dressed in dog-tooth check and breeches made from finest Donegal tweed. It was probably this which led George Bernard Shaw to quip that the 1921 team members looked 'like a picnic party in Connemara surprised by a snowstorm'.

Climbing equipment employed on the mountain itself was similarly *ad hoc* and unspecialised. Single-skin nailed leather boots would offer little in the way of insulation, while the long-handled ice-axes and hemp ropes employed by the climbers had scarcely changed

in design for a century. The reconnaissance climbing was also undertaken without bottled oxygen. This was mainly because the equipment available was still in its infancy (Kellas planned to conduct research during the expedition in order to develop the technology later), but also because of considerable resistance within the British climbing establishment (including Mallory), and the feeling that the use of supplementary oxygen was in some way unsporting. It was yet another of the many ethical dilemmas which has preoccupied British climbing down the years.

Given the rudimentary equipment, the relative inexperience of the participants and the myriad personality clashes that attended the expedition, the achievements of the 1921 reconnaissance were remarkable. Guy Bullock, with the surveyor, Wheeler and three of their strongest porters climbed to the *North Col* at a height of 6,700m and could see no obstacles ahead to bar them reaching the summit another time along the *North East Ridge*. Too late for this expedition, they discovered that the key to approaching the *North Col* more directly lay in the long East Rongbuk Glacier. Other valuable lessons learned included the fact that the summer monsoon months were no time to be tackling a Himalayan peak like Everest. The continual heavy snowfall made conditions extremely difficult and often suicidally dangerous.

On the negative side, the expedition suffered a death (Dr Kellas on the approach march), and much illness (including the climbing leader, the irascible Harold Raeburn who had to miss most of the expedition, much to everyone's relief). Nonetheless, the team had proved there was a feasible way up the mountain and had gained much-needed experience.

The following year, Mallory was back, as part of the much larger follow-up expedition. He and Morshead remained from the original team, augmented by new members, including leader General Bruce, his nephew, Geoffrey Bruce, expedition photographer Captain John Noel, climbers Howard Somervell and Edward Norton and the brilliant but maverick Australian alpinist George Finch, who had been excluded from the reconnaissance trip 'on health grounds'. Finch brooded darkly that it may have had more to do with his perceived status as an outsider. He was officially selected as an expedition scientist, in charge of the new-fangled oxygen apparatus, which would be trialled fully for the first time. There was considerable resistance, nevertheless, to the introduction of such cheating, not least by George Mallory himself.

The expedition struggled against poor weather and illness throughout May. A near disaster was averted by Mallory's prompt ice-axe belay on snow slopes at 7,925m when Morshead slipped pulling off Somervell and Norton. Their luck did not hold two weeks later when a snow slope avalanched, killing seven Sherpas.

On the positive side, though, the 1922 expedition set a new altitude record with Finch and Geoffrey Bruce's attainment of 8,320m, proving the efficacy of the oxygen apparatus. On the darker side, the loss of so many lives was a bitter blow, and many were to blame Mallory directly for picking a route up a clearly avalanche-prone slope.

There were mutterings about his carelessness, exemplified by Tom Longstaff's cutting remark that, 'Mallory is a good, stout hearted baby, but quite unfit to be placed in charge of anything, including himself'.

'English air'
Early attempts at using bottled oxygen

The first recorded use of supplementary oxygen as an aid to high-altitude mountaineering occurred on Arnold Mumm's expedition to the Indian Garhwal in 1907. He took a few small bottles with him on an exploratory journey to Trisul but the concept was well before its time and most of his companions considered the idea laughable.

The mountaineering physiologist Alexander Kellas pioneered studies into altitude sickness and acclimatisation. He carried out experiments in a decompression chamber and arranged to do practical work in the field on **Kamet** (7,756m) in 1920, although the apparatus was delayed by the shipping authorities classifying it as 'high explosives'. Kellas had a programme of experiments prepared for Everest 1921 (on which he was the oxygen officer). On his death, however, no-one else was familiar enough with the apparatus to test it.

By the second Everest expedition of 1922, the technology had developed sufficiently for oxygen sets to be tried seriously. Systems had been developed at Oxford University for the RAF by Professor Dreyer. His opinion on the necessity of the equipment at altitude was uncompromising. 'I do not think you will get up without it,' he told George Finch, 'but if you do succeed you may not get down again.' Even so the equipment was very heavy (14.5kg), bulky and unreliable, and there was considerable resist-

ance to the idea from many climbers on the grounds that it constituted cheating. Everest climbers and the committee split into pro-oxygen and anti-oxygen factions. Although eventually won over, George Mallory was initially firmly in the 'anti' camp; arguing that the use of 'English air' (a term coined by the bemused Sherpas) diluted the purity of man's struggle against nature.

Although the gas enthusiasts were eventually to be proved correct, they had to put up with a huge amount of barracking by the oxygen antagonists, exemplified by the acerbic comments of the secretary of the Mount Everest Committee, the scabrous Hinks: 'This afternoon we go to see a gas drill. They have contrived a most wonderful apparatus which will make you die laughing...'

Nevertheless, 10 sets were taken to Everest in 1922. Even though only three eventually worked, and the high point of the attempt was undertaken by Norton without supplementary oxygen, it was gradually recognised, even by die-hards like Mallory, that 'English air' could help in the attempts to climb the mountain, so it was here to stay.

Mallory *(left)*, Norton and Somervell *(photographer)* climbed without oxygen equipment to just below 8,230m on 21st May, 1922

George Finch in 1922 testing the first oxygen apparatus used on an attempt on Everest

Vanquishing
none but ourselves

The epic of
Mallory & Irvine

(1924)

The 1924 Expedition – *standing from left to right:* Irvine, Mallory, Norton, Odell, MacDonald (trade agent); *seated:* Shebbeare, G. Bruce, Somervell, Beetham

The events of the 1924 expedition would make Mallory the most famous mountaineer of all time, while his disappearance with Andrew 'Sandy' Irvine into the eternal mists, dramatically 'going strong for the top' would lead to endless speculation over their fate by climbing historians for the rest of the twentieth century.

The Mount Everest Committee had decided to have another go at climbing the peak and the Tibetan government were cajoled once more into giving permission. As with the previous expeditions, the old boy network heavily influenced team selection. A hard core of experienced members were invited from the 1922 expedition, but the individualistic Finch was unceremoniously dropped to be replaced by a fresh-faced youth of 21 who had considerable rowing expertise, but comparatively little climbing experience: Andrew 'Sandy' Irvine. Joining him was Lakeland rock-climber Bentley Beetham, John de Vars Hazard, and geologist Noel Odell.

Mallory, prevaricated. He wanted to spend more time with his young wife and family and was tired of the almost mechanical process of attempting the peak again. Eventually he succumbed to the powerful idea of the summit, also aware that his future financial security might yet rest on cementing his reputation as the conqueror of Everest.

Mallory's penultimate message to Odell. Sent from Camp VI and received by Odell at Camp V at about 6 p.m. 6th June, 1924

The plan for 1924 was to place three progressively higher camps along the ridge from the *North Col* occupied by climbers, some using bottled oxygen and some without, leading to a series of two-man attempts on the final summit slopes. Unfortunately, the weather did not stick to the schedule and a series of storms caused several epics, during which porters were nearly killed after being marooned in a camp above avalanche-prone slopes. The debilitating effects of the weather ground the team down and by early June the expedition was almost completely exhausted.

Nevertheless, a camp was established at nearly 8,230m and Norton and Somervell set out to attempt the summit. Somervell was forced to turn back as he was having breathing

Andrew 'Sandy' Irvine with oxygen apparatus. Everest Base Camp 1924

Norton, Somervell and the Sherpas with whom they 'went high' in 1924

difficulties (he unknowingly had frostbite in his larynx), but Norton ploughed on solo, reaching an incredible 8,573m – and all without supplementary oxygen. Unfortunately, it was at considerable cost; he was now suffering from double vision and stuck on dangerous outward-sloping slabs covered in powder snow.

"My eye trouble was getting worse and was a severe handicap. I had perhaps 200ft [60m] or more of this nasty going to surmount before I emerged on the north face of the final pyramid. It was now 1p.m. and a brief calculation showed that I had no chance of climbing the remaining 800 or 900ft [240m or 270m] if I was to return in safety."

Norton carefully picked his way down to rejoin the ailing Somervell and returned to the *North Col*, but not before Somervell had almost

choked to death before managing to cough up a large section of the skin lining of his throat.

Most thought the expedition was finished. Everyone was weary and they had given it their best shot, with Norton's magnificent and futuristic solo climb. But Mallory pleaded with Norton to let him have one last-ditch attempt to climb the summit with the relatively inexperienced 22-year old Oxford Rowing Blue, 'Sandy' Irvine.

Mallory also chose to use oxygen, thereby reversing his previous antipathy towards this artificial aid. However, the expedition had been incredibly physically draining: Mallory clearly felt he was going to need all the help he could get on this final effort. Norton, suffering by now from snow-blindness (the result of removing his dark glasses to concentrate on the tricky slabs of his high point), was worried about the wisdom of climbing with such an inexperienced mountaineer as Irvine, but did not have the energy to argue with Mallory. Nevertheless, he had grave doubts, 'There is no doubt Mallory knows he is leading a forlorn hope,' he told John Noel.

Mallory and Irvine trudged back up to the top camp in preparation for their summit bid, while Noel Odell spent the evening in the camp below. The following morning Odell thought he saw the summit party moving slowly upwards, but owing to drifting cloud unfortunately he was unable to locate their position relative to the summit with any degree of precision.

The resulting confusion has allowed historians to argue ever since over whether the duo may have reached the top or not.

The only thing not open to debate is that, as Odell watched two specks climb upwards into the clouds, it would be the last time George Mallory and Sandy Irvine would be seen alive.

The last known picture of Mallory and Irvine: leaving Camp IV for their final summit attempt on 6th June, 1924

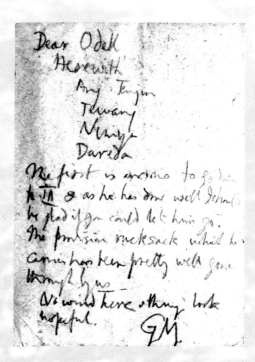

Mallory's last message to Odell. Sent from Camp VI and received by Odell at Camp V at about 3 p.m. 7th June, 1924

Andrew 'Sandy' Irvine
(1902–1924)

Like Mallory, Sandy Irvine came from a solidly respectable middle-class family in Cheshire, but in many ways that was where the similarities ended. Unlike the absent-minded, intellectually inclined Mallory, Irvine (seventeen years his junior) was an athletically enthusiastic all-round good egg, with a practical aptitude for solving mechanical problems. The difference in their mountaineering and life experiences was vast.

Mallory was an ace rock-climber who had survived alpine epics, service in the Great War and encounters with various homosexual Bohemians at Magdalene College. Irvine was an Oxford rowing blue who had been on a sledging expedition to Spitzbergen but who possessed limited mountaineering experience. Despite the contrasts, the duo gelled well on Everest and have gone down as the most famous mountaineering pairing in history after Hillary and Tenzing.

Irvine's selection for the 1924 expedition came about by chance, thanks to his making the acquaintance of Everest veteran Noel Odell during rowing practice at Putney. Odell was looking to recruit suitable candidates for an Oxford University sledging trip to Spitzbergen in 1923 and invited the solidly-built oarsman along. During the expedition Odell took a shine to Irvine, impressed by his natural bonhomie and the fact that he was good at fiddling with bits of machinery – an important talent given the reliance placed by the pioneering Everest expeditions on the new-fangled oxygen apparatus. In the eyes of Odell, Irvine's background, education and rowing achievements indicated he was clearly a team player and 'one of us'. He was an ideal replacement, therefore, for the individualistic

Australian George Finch whom the Mount Everest Committee was keen to be rid of for the 1924 attempt.

On Everest, Sandy Irvine performed strongly despite his relative inexperience, hefting heavy loads about the slopes like a Trojan, fixing just about every piece of equipment that broke and performing miracles of tinkering with the temperamental oxygen equipment. It was these attributes, along with Irvine's undoubted fitness that most likely led Mallory to choose him to accompany him on the final summit attempt, passing over the more obviously qualified Noel Odell. The latter was renowned for being rather slow and methodical – characteristics which would undoubtedly have tested the patience of the famously impetuous Mallory. A young blood like Irvine who possessed the added advantage of actually knowing how to keep the vital bottled oxygen flowing must have presented an overwhelming advantage to a man keen to get on with bagging the summit as fast as possible. Whether or not Irvine had any say in the matter is yet another question which remains unsolved after he and Mallory disappeared into the clouds on June 8th 1924.

Hidden
Himalaya
(1930–1939)

Left: Nanda Devi (7,824m)

Organising expeditions
on the **back of an envelope**

The unlikely pairing of Shipton and Tilman

Although the fight for Everest continued to grab all the headlines during the 1930s, out of the limelight, two Britons were quietly getting on with the exploration of the rest of the Himalaya and Karakoram.

In the annals of exploratory mountaineering Shipton and Tilman stand head and shoulders above the rest, thanks to their zest for mountain travel and the economical and understated, manner in which they achieved it. Although both men were also heavily involved in attempts to climb **Everest** (8,850m), they were happiest operating away from the publicity and glamour of that mountain; their preferred *modus operandi* being the low-key, highly-mobile exploratory expedition to a little known area. Indeed, the modern phrase 'doing more with less' might have been coined by Eric Shipton and Bill Tilman, two very different characters who nevertheless shared a common trait: the ability to 'organise a Himalayan expedition in half an hour on the back of an envelope.'

The most successful mountaineering pairing of the 1930s began in an unlikely spot – a Kenyan coffee plantation. Frustrated alpinist Eric Shipton was pottering about on a colonial farm in Africa in 1929 and feeling rather bored when he met down-to-earth grump Bill Tilman. Shipton was 22, dashingly handsome, sociable, and developing into quite a ladies' man. Tilman was ten years older, a distinguished war veteran, and a confirmed bachelor with curmudgeonly instincts. It should have been a disaster; instead it was a climbing partnership made in heaven.

Mount Kenya (5,199m) seen from the Teleki Valley to the south west

Tilman's common-sensical personality, together with his laconic dry wit proved the perfect foil to Shipton's more romantic, garrulous character. The pair's first climb was typically audacious; the first traverse of the spiky exposed ridge between Mount Kenya's highest summits. Shipton's reputation as a mountaineer, which had already been growing as a result of a previous ascent of **Mount Kenya** (5,199m) with fellow colonial Percy Wyn-Harris, was cemented by this climb. As a consequence, he was invited to join Frank Smythe's expedition to the Himalayan peak of **Kamet** (7,756m) in 1931, where he was one of the four team members that successfully summited.

The experience opened Shipton's eyes to the huge untapped potential of exploratory mountaineering and travel in the Himalaya and whetted his appetite for more. He was duly invited to take part in the ultimately unsuccessful 1933 Everest attempt – an experience which left him with grave reservations about the value of large-scale expeditions.

Tilman, meanwhile, in typically idiosyncratic fashion, had decided to return to Britain by

Rishi Ganga Gorge

bicycling nearly 5,000km across the neck of Africa ('a most cheap and efficacious method'). In a hint of what was to come on his and Shipton's notoriously spartan expeditions, he lived mainly off roasted bananas. Back in Britain, Tilman resumed correspondence with Shipton, sending a letter suggesting they meet up for a fortnight's rock climbing in the Lake District. By return of post Shipton suggested another plan: a seven-month exploratory climbing expedition to the Himalaya. Unfazed by this startlingly radical alternative, Tilman readily agreed, and thus began the main phase of one of the most celebrated partnerships in mountaineering.

Shipton's plan was to attempt to enter the awe-inspiring and unexplored Nanda Devi Sanctuary of the Indian Garhwal by means of the fabulously remote and seemingly impenetrable Rishi Ganga Gorge. He had become fascinated by this challenge after talking with veteran Himalayan explorer, Tom Longstaff, who had tried in vain to enter the beautiful sanctuary 27 years before. The gorge itself had repelled several competent and lavishly-equipped expeditions. Shipton and Tilman's approach was to eschew such profligacy and keep it simple. To them, items such as tea and sugar were regarded as luxury items, and their main food supplies (based on the simple formula of two pounds of food per man per day) comprised flour, rice and the local clarified butter, ghee. Their equipment consisted of two small tents, kerosene stoves, ropes, cameras and survey instruments, candle lanterns and matches. For protection against the elements each man took a light windproof suit, sweaters, woollen trousers, a balaclava, puttees, socks, a down sleeping bag, climbing boots and an ice-axe.

With an almost ascetic stoicism the two men, together with their porters, battled for day after day up the precipitous, jungled sides of the gigantic ravine, finding improbable ways past crumbling vertical walls and slimy, overhanging slabs. Disaster struck at one point, when Tilman lost his pipe during a river crossing. Without this he could become even more irascible than normal. Luckily, Shipton had recently taken up smoking, so the two men shared the one pipe for the remainder of the journey and disaster was averted. After three weeks of effort they broke through into the Sanctuary – the first people to do so – and beheld the majestic spire of **Nanda Devi** (7,824m) towering above herds of tame mountain sheep grazing on pasture strewn with a riotous alpine flora.

The party spent several weeks surveying and mapping the newly discovered terrain, climbing satellite peaks of about 6,400m, before embarking on an equally epic journey west across the Badrinath Range where they spent a further two months battling through monsoon-drenched bamboo forest, and almost running out of food before breaking through to the other side. However, Shipton considered it worth the effort:

"We were the first outside the pages of Hindu mythology to effect a direct connection between the three main sources of the sacred River Ganges".

As if this was not enough they then returned to the Nanda Devi Sanctuary to complete their survey, before ending the expedition with a spectacular finale, finding an audacious exit over the mountainous rim which involved abseiling

Eric **Shipton** (1907–1977)

Keeping it simple

Summing up an incredible life of adventure in a nutshell, climbing historian Paul Nunn described Eric Shipton as 'a romantic-individualist, nomadically adventuring in an end-of-Empire globe'. Although Shipton was born into a comparatively well-off colonial middle-class family on a tea-plantation in Sri Lanka, he was never to be financially well-off himself, thanks to the conscious decision not to mortgage his active years against a comfortable retirement.

His interest in travel may have been partly genetic (his mother was an inveterate traveller) and his path towards an alternative lifestyle probably began at public school when he became hooked on mountaineering after visiting the Alps. A failure to pass the entrance examinations for Cambridge (Shipton suffered from dyslexia which hampered his written performance) probably sealed his fate.

Instead of enduring further torture in classrooms, and anxious to escape the formal constraints of conventional society, the restless Shipton headed out to the colonies, ending up on a coffee plantation in Kenya. Nevertheless, he had not abandoned thoughts of alpine arêtes and glaciers, and optimistically packed both ice-axe and rope, which he secretly admitted seemed rather ridiculous in the heart of Africa.

It was just as well he did, for it was here that he came across Bill Tilman, a meeting which would change the course of both their lives.

After pioneering new routes on **Mount Kenya** (5,199m) they would spend much of the 1930s climbing and exploring in the Himalaya and Karakoram, employing their revolutionary lightweight approach to mountain travel, and eschewing the conventional wisdom of bloated, military-scale expeditions.

For a while there seemed to be no stopping them and they roamed the length and breadth of these ranges, bagging peaks, but specialising in monster exploratory glacier journeys. As a result of this activity, Shipton and Tilman are often credited with inventing the notion of the lightweight expedition; they were famous for minimal planning and living largely off rice, butter and flour. It is ironic therefore, that outside of mountaineering circles, Shipton became famous chiefly for his rôle in leading old-fashioned siege-style military assaults on Everest. But Shipton's heart lay in low-key exploratory mountaineering, and he was never happier than when pushing new ground over unexplored passes and valley systems. It may well be that it was this hippyish lack of enthusiasm for the over-organised expedition, which contributed to his being unceremoniously and humiliatingly dumped from leadership of the (ultimately successful) 1953 Everest trip. Although this was a crushing blow to his pride, it ensured Shipton went on to pursue what he felt were far more interesting small expeditions to Patagonia.

Personally, Shipton was a striking character. With his astonishing blue eyes and charisma, he was never short of suitors from the opposite sex. (One smitten lover remembers meeting Shipton at a garden party; 'I melted like an ice cube and fell hook line and sinker for him.'). He had a whole string of romances throughout his life, and although he did get married, had two sons and later divorced, such was his charm he seems to have managed to have kept on extremely friendly terms with most of his past loves. It was probably inevitable that he could never commit himself to a permanent relationship given his restless, nomadic nature, plus the fact that, as the mother of one of his girlfriends remarked: 'This man's a dreamer and just lives on a glacier. What good is he to my daughter?'

He also overcame his dyslexia to become an accomplished writer, documenting his life and travels in many books which have become mountaineering classics. Shipton's writings showcase his personality perfectly, dealing as they do mostly with his main love: the small, intimate wide-ranging mountain expedition. Through all of them runs Shipton's gently ironic, understated style, always putting the mountains, landscape and his companions in the foreground while he, the narrator, modestly hovers in the background.

Bill **Tilman** (1898–1977)

Adventure ahoy!

Professional grump Bill Tilman, the perfect foil to suave Eric Shipton, was a remarkable man of action who continues to inspire generations of adventurers. Not only did he succeed in 1936 in climbing the highest peak then attained (Nanda Devi – 7,824m), a record he held for 14 years, but he fought in two World Wars and was parachuted behind enemy lines in the Balkans at the age of 45 to organise resistance against the German occupation.

As he got older, rather than retiring to a well-earned pipe-and-slippers rest, he turned to exploring the remoter mountains of the world using ancient sea-going barques, several of which sank amongst ice-floes, leading to major epics. To top it all, he was a wonderful, understated writer, describing his adventures with a wit so dry sparrows could bathe in it.

His greatest mountaineering triumph on Nanda Devi was all the more exceptional given that he perennially suffered from altitude sickness and was poor at acclimatising. Partly because of this, but mainly because he preferred solitude and exploration to the crowded, grinding routine of large-scale climbing expeditions, Tilman preferred the lightweight treks across high passes and untrodden glaciers equally favoured by his pal Shipton, and which made their partnership so fruitful. Nevertheless Tilman had a (partly undeserved) reputation as a morose, misogynistic curmudgeon.

A quote from his closest friend and long-time climbing companion, Eric Shipton, illustrates their odd-couple relationship perfectly:

'How I hated Tilman in the early morning. Not only on that expedition, but on all the years we have been together. He never slept like an ordinary person. Whatever time we agreed to awake, long before (how long I never knew) he would slide from his sleeping bag and start stirring his silly porridge over the Primus stove. I used gradually to become aware of this irritating noise and would bury my head in silent rage against the preposterous injustice of being wakened half an hour too soon. When his filthy brew was ready he would say 'Show a leg,' or some such imbecile remark. In moments of triumph on top of a peak I have gone so far as to admit that our presence there was due in large measure to this quality of Tilman's, but in the dark hours before dawn such an admission of virtue in my companion has never touched the fringe of my consciousness.'

Nevertheless, he inspired tremendous loyalty in others and is regarded by many as the last great hero of the twentieth century.

As befits this status he died with his sea-boots on, disappearing without trace aged 80 (along with the boat on which he was sailing and the rest of the crew) in the treacherous southern waters of the Antarctic Convergence.

from ice bollards and dodging avalanches 'in a day of toil over-packed with thrills'.

Despite the adventures, risks and pipes they had shared, the pair couldn't help retaining a high degree of middle-class English reserve. 'As we had done in Africa', wrote Shipton, 'we continued to address one another as "Tilman" and "Shipton"; and when, after another seven months continuously together, I suggested that it was time he called me "Eric", he became acutely embarrassed, hung his head and muttered, "It sounds so damned silly"'.

In 1935, Shipton was invited to lead a reconnaissance expedition to Everest. Although the prospect of Everest seemed to hold a stark contrast to the mobile, carefree exploratory trip he had just completed, Shipton's basic philosophy was undimmed. 'I had a private motive', he later wrote, 'my dislike of massive mountaineering expeditions had become something of an obsession, and I was anxious for the opportunity to demonstrate that, for one-tenth of the former cost and with a fraction of bother, a party… could make a strong summit attempt'. He naturally asked his comrade-in-arms, Tilman, to join his team of six climbers, thinking he would be delighted. His initial reaction was quite the reverse.

Tilman had his heart set on returning to Nanda Devi and attempting that beautiful and elegant peak, rather than the trench-war attrition inevitable on the pitiless wind-blown slopes of the *North Col*. 'Though he did not say so,' said Shipton, 'I suspected the root of his objection was that, while he had been forced to accept the stark necessity of my company, the prospect of having five companions was scarcely tolerable'. Nevertheless they both went to try their luck reconnoitring the mountain. The following year, 1936, Shipton was invited to Hugh Ruttledge's expedition, this time to try for the summit. Although Shipton succumbed, Tilman had had enough and the two climbers went their separate ways: Shipton to an ultimately frustrating expedition to Everest and Tilman to complete a phenomenally successful ascent of Nanda Devi (which at 7,824m was to hold the record as the highest climbed peak in the world until 1950).

Tilman's trip, undertaken as a joint Anglo-American expedition with a couple of veteran members of the Alpine Club and a bunch of fresh-faced sophomores from Harvard, was conducted with the usual abstemious stoicism. The Americans, initially taken aback by their eccentric older English partners, grew to appreciate the idiosyncratic wisdom of their leader, and both sides were amused by the sharp cultural differences thrown up by the two sides. American member Charlie Houston remembers, 'The Brits didn't know what to make of us Yanks and had some difficulty understanding our form of the language we were supposed to share. True to form, Tilman said nothing, but looked wary'.

Later on it was the Yanks' turn to laugh: 'The entire supply of tea fell down the steep snow slope; frantic search was unproductive and the Brits were devastated. There was serious talk of going home, but we were quite happy with our Ovaltine and insisted on continuing'. The expedition turned out to be an exceptionally happy and successful one. Tilman overcame his normal acclimatisation problems to achieve Nanda Devi's summit together with

Noel Odell, a man who had been rejected for the 1930s Everest expeditions because he was regarded by the committee as not fit enough. It was a moment of personal triumph for both of them and a ringing vindication of the Shipton-Tilman lightweight approach. Even so, English reserve demanded decorum on the summit. 'I believe we so far forgot ourselves as to shake hands on it', recorded a shame-faced Tilman.

Shipton was delighted by his friend's success and the pair re-united in 1937 for another monster mountain exploration journey. This time, Shipton planned to traverse some of the wildest and most uncharted ranges of the world: the Karakoram. This area of arid, almost desert-like mountains extends westwards from the main Himalayan chain, straddling the borders of what is now Pakistan, China and the former Soviet Union. It contains the second highest peak in the world, **K2** (8,611m), and holds the world's biggest glaciers outside the polar regions. Although the southern part of this area was partly-charted, albeit little-visited, what really attracted Shipton were the large letters printed over the northern half of the latest maps, which read simply: '*Unexplored*'.

Over four months, Shipton and Tilman's party, accompanied by the brilliant but artistically temperamental scientists Michael Spender and John Auden (both brothers of famous poets), would travel completely self-sufficiently, mapping and surveying vast tracts of mountain range and glacier system. They travelled up the Baltoro Glacier, past K2, crossing giant meltwater streams using rafts constructed from inflated sheep's bladders, photographed the fearsomely spiky **Trango Towers** (6,286m), noted the mighty **Mustagh Tower** (7,273m), **Gasherbrum** (8,068m) and **Broad Peak**

Trango Towers (6,286m)

(8,048m), and crossed the Central Asian Divide. They pressed on into the Shaksgam River, hemmed in by weird Dolomitic towers of limestone, and paused to take stock of the situation. 'East and west of us,' wrote Shipton, 'stretched an unexplored section, 80 miles [128km] long, of the greatest watershed in the world. We had food enough to keep us alive for three months in this place of my dreams. I wanted nothing more.' They spent three weeks exploring the surrounding valley systems, crossing back over the treacherous Shaksgam River, now in full mid-summer flood, and struck south up the K2 glacier. The final part of their mammoth peregrination saw them travel west to penetrate the high passes of the Karakoram. Splitting into three groups, Shipton and Spender headed north to the Braldu Glacier and Shimshal Pass

The **Karakoram**

The Karakoram comprises a huge complex of high mountains running parallel to, but lying mostly to the north and west of the Himalaya. The peaks, which straddle numerous borders, some of which are still disputed, traverse the territories of Pakistan, India, Afghanistan and China. A land of superlatives, it contains the largest glaciers outside the polar regions as well as the second highest mountain in the world, **K2** (8,611m), just one of 19 peaks above 7,600m in height.

Unlike the Himalaya, the valleys are arid semi-desert with an average rainfall of less than 250mm per year, but the permanent snows of the high peaks and glaciers provide copious meltwater for intricate irrigation and the major valleys are green with barley field, poplar groves and apricot orchards. The climbing, which draws many expeditions from all over the world, ranges from giant 8,000m snow peaks such as **Broad Peak** (8,047m), to soaring spires of granite such as the **Trango Towers** (6,286m).

Left: K2 – the second highest mountain in the world at 8,611m and the highest peak in the Karakoram

and thence to the autonomous kingdom of Hunza. Tilman and two Sherpas headed west to the huge snow bowl of Snow Lake at the head of the giant Hispar Glacier, proving it was not an ice cap motherlode which fed all the glaciers of the region, but just another normal glacier. He then pressed on south to the village of Askole and the end of the expedition. It had been a magnificent achievement, completed at a fraction of the cost an undertaking of such magnitude would normally involve (Shipton spent a measly £840 on the whole thing, all in, door-to-door). However, there hadn't been enough climbing for Tilman's taste. 'We have had very little climbing – only two peaks of about 20,000ft [6,111m]. they were both difficult and gave good days, but hardly worth coming all this way for', was his grumpy verdict. Worse still, Tilman was always rather contemptuous of the 'scientific' justification for mountaineering expeditions, and thought it got in the way of the climbing. On one occasion when they dropped a theodolite while lowering it on a rope, Shipton remarked of his friend,

> *"He showed great self-restraint in not*
> *encouraging it to fall the rest of the way."*

It was partly this divergence of priorities – Shipton's increasing interest in pure mountain travel and survey, as opposed to Tilman's keenness to go up peaks rather than just past them – that would soon lead to the eventual dissolution of their classic partnership.

In the meantime however, they were still together and the following year, the pair were back on Everest, this time Shipton swapping the leadership with Tilman. Although they had as much success with a small-scale expedition as any of the large, military-scale predecessors, the usual bugbear, poor weather, resulted ultimately in defeat. Shipton began organising another mammoth Karakoram exploration for 1939 but Tilman, weary of science and survey, and patriotically aware that there might soon be a war, stayed in Britain, wanting to be ready to serve his country. Shipton commenced his Karakoram expedition, but it was cut short by the war, as Tilman had predicted.

Shipton went on to become His Majesty's Consul-General in Kashgar during the war, got entangled with Everest again after the war, and continued to undertake lightweight exploratory mountaineering trips to Patagonia well into his 60s.

Tilman had an eventful war, leading partisans in the Balkans before beginning a new and long career as a sailor-mountaineer exploring outlandish polar islands.

He died with his sea boots on, disappearing in a storm in the South Atlantic in 1977. Despite their great individual endeavours, it is as the far-seeing 1930s partnership which advocated a 'small is beautiful' approach to climbing the biggest mountains that they will remain most remembered. Ironically, it would not be until the 1970s that their philosophy would be taken up seriously by a new generation, following a couple of decades of enormously expensive, high-profile expeditions which would dominate activity in the Greater Ranges.

Above: Looking north-west down the upper Baltoro Glacier towards Mitre Peak (left) Concordia and Mustagh Tower (7,273m)

Below: These days the Hispar Glacier is often crossed on skis

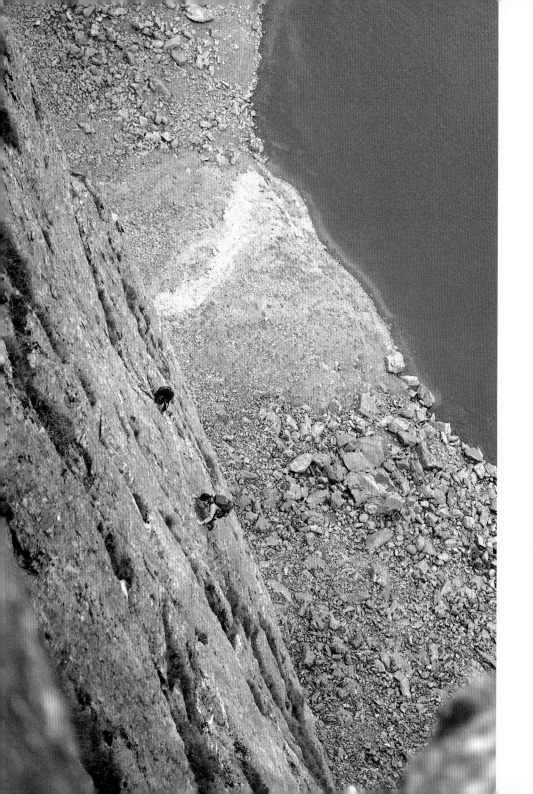

Regaining
the Heights
(1920–1940)

Retrenchment
(1918–1928)

The events of the Great War of 1914–1918 were to mark the nascent sport of rock climbing as indelibly as any other aspect of British society. The carnage had removed an entire cohort of young climbers from the cutting edge of the rock face, among them the brilliant Siegfried Herford, pioneer of the hardest climb in the country: *Central Buttress*. Herford symbolised a kind of lost generation of British climbers, whose potential would now never be fully realised. In their place was simply the mountaineers' war memorial of Great Gable in the Lake District, which the Fell & Rock Climbing Club purchased to commemorate their fallen members. It came to represent all those climbers who had left their home crags for the last time in the summer of 1914. The trauma of the war thus meant a break in continuity, stalling the startlingly rapid progress made by the new adventure sport. It required the maturing of a new wave of climbers before standards would once again begin their upward rise.

Below: *Clogwyn Du'r Arddu* or 'Cloggy' as it is known to climbers

The **new wave** (1928–1940)

By the end of the 1920s a core of young hard climbers had begun to form. An important strand of this group was supplied by the ever-active Oxbridge mountaineering clubs. From Cambridge came the likes of Jack Longland, Ivan Waller and Alf Bridge who were to start climbing athletic and challenging new rock lines, especially in the Peak District and Wales. Longland is perhaps most associated with the exploration of daring new mountain lines in Snowdonia where, although he did not realise it at the time, his bold 1930 route *Javelin Blade*, was one of the first rock climbs of the futuristically difficult 'Extreme' grade. The confidence of the new climbers was such that they began to venture onto big, steep, intimidating mountain cliffs which the previous generation had regarded as too difficult. One of these was Snowdon's stupendous northern crag of *Clogwyn Du'r Arddu*. The rocks here are organised into two huge buttresses and the solving of their intricate and frightening problems became an obsessive addiction for the new élite.

Together with Longland in the forefront of this band was a brilliantly gifted climber from Liverpool, Colin Kirkus. It was Kirkus who is said to have coined the climber's moniker for the cliff of 'Cloggy', but he also left more than a nomenclatural imprint. Kirkus pioneered the breathtakingly exposed climb up the cliff's *Great Slab* and added several more improbable

lines to both this and other Welsh cliffs. All were consistently of the highest levels of difficulty of the day. Kirkus also exemplifies another trend in British climbing during the inter-war period, in that he was not particularly restricted to one geographical area. The wider availability of motorised transport (for those who could afford it) and the expansion of the club hut system meant that climbers were more likely to rove around the UK's mountain ranges.

Few were as extreme as Graham Macphee, who wrote a rock-climbers' guide to Ben Nevis while living in Liverpool, but many emulated Kirkus, who was pioneering difficult new routes in both Wales and the Lake District, such as his superb climbs on Scafell's steep *East Buttress*.

Fellows and Amazons
The rise of working-class and women climbers

Another phenomenon of great significance during the mid-1930s was the beginning of working-class participation in climbing. Since the 1920s, the social background of most climbers, although broadening, was still largely middle-class, and professional in nature, with a tendency towards 'clubbability'. To be a member of one of the main British climbing clubs in the inter-war period still usually meant you were more likely to be a doctor, a lawyer or a university lecturer than a sheet-metal worker or joiner. It was also still overwhelmingly a male-dominated scene.

By the mid-30s, however, the vanguard of what was to become the post-war proletarian invasion of climbing appeared, and this also

coincided with the increasing involvement of women in the sport. The growth of institutions like the youth hostelling movement was helping to introduce more people of limited means to the open spaces, while widespread unemployment also began to emphasise the maxim that 'at both ends of the social spectrum there is a leisure class'. North of the border Jock Nimlin and some of his Glasgow contemporaries began visiting the Cobbler, the rocky peak within easy reach of the city, living rough under boulders or howffs and putting up new rock climbs while remaining resolutely outside of the established club network. Instead, penurious climbers began forming their own, less formal associations, such as the *Creagh Dhu* in Scotland, or the *Sheffield Climbing Club* in south Yorkshire where new pioneers like Frank Elliot were putting up gritstone routes of the highest technical standards by the early '30s despite a poverty of material equipment. 'None of them could afford proper climbing gear', recorded Peak climbing historian Eric Byne, 'they often wore workmen's overalls or cast-off plus fours bought for a song in the city's rag-market. A good rope was a treasure, worn-out ropes were passed down and used until the very threads curled up in disdain.'

In the Lake District, Langdale quarryman Jim Birkett began climbing, first of all in his working clogs and then using more conventional nailed boots. Having developed exceptionally strong fingers and hands from riving rocks in the quarry, Birkett employed them to good effect when he started putting up ever more difficult and bold climbs in the Lake District, which were soon amongst the hardest in the land.

Elsewhere, Workington miner Bill Peascod was also making his mark with a series of bold, pioneering climbs on the western Lakeland fells around Buttermere, cycling to the crags after a nightshift to swap coal face for rock face.

In Kendal, two working-class employees of K Shoes, Sid Cross and Alice Nelson joined together to make a formidable climbing team on both rock and ice. Together they made some exceptional ascents in the Lake District and Scotland.

The appearance of Alice 'Jammy' Nelson on the scene also marked the arrival of women at the leading edge of British climbing. She was not only the first woman to lead the still-revered *Central Buttress* of Scafell Crag but also the first woman to lead Grade V snow and ice climbs during the pair's ambitious winter ascents of *Bowfell Buttress* and Scafell's *Steep Gill*.

Outdoor emancipation
The formation of the Pinnacle Club

Although the arrival of Alice Nelson on the scene marked a dramatic rise in the standard of women's lead climbing, the profile of female participation within the domestic sport had been steadily rising since the Great War. The formation of the Pinnacle Club in 1921 was an affirmation that late nineteenth century feminist principles had at last penetrated the hitherto gentlemanly domain of climbing.

Largely the brainchild of the charismatic Pat Kelly, the Pinnacle Club was the world's first true national women's club: a point deliberately rammed home by the omission of the hitherto conventional, but qualifying adjective 'lady' from their title. Indeed, unlike the already

The Pinnacle Club was founded in 1921

established *Ladies'* Scottish and *Ladies'* Alpine clubs (both effectively junior affiliates of the senior male organisations) members of the Pinnacle Club remained resolutely independent of the enemy species and preferred to climb as all-female ropes.

This was controversial: 'In those days, even in the Lakes, a girl couldn't walk about in villages in climbing clothes without hard stares from the women and sniggers from the louts', recalled founding member Dorothy Pilley. The pioneer club members weren't really that unconventional however; in many ways they were a small group of middle-class tomboys with short-cropped hair who were in the habit of calling each other by surnames or nicknames. In fact it sounds very much like a continuation of the Angela Brazil-era private girls' schools from which many of them hailed. Nevertheless, despite this semi-conformist atmosphere, the PC really was quite radical in concept, establishing as it did the principle of encouraging the development of women's climbing without having to be second on the rope lurking in the shadow of a male leader.

Scotland
The icemen cometh
(1930–1940)

In Scotland, partly isolated from the mainstream of English and Welsh climbing and resolutely ploughing its own path until after the Second World War, the situation in the 1920s was even more dire than south of the border.

One of the leading Scottish climbers of the 1930s, Bill Murray, went as far as to state that, 'in the 1920s climbing in Scotland was to all appearances dead'. Much the same reason lay behind the recession: the fact that many of the most promising young climbers, such as Charles Inglis Clarke, had been killed in the war.

However, unlike the Lakeland situation, which possessed some residual continuity, the stifling of information and experience was compounded by the attitude of the increasingly stuffy and moribund Scottish Mountaineering Club, which effectively discouraged new blood by maintaining a culture of élitism.

There was really no-one around to lead by example until the emergence of the great exploratory climber, J.H.B. Bell and the Ben Nevis *aficionado*, G.G. Macphee, in the '30s. The consequence was that it never occurred to Murray and his youthful peers that

"… our performance was handicapped by an unnatural generation gap – one so deep and wide that we could not imagine that some of our predecessors might have achieved standards beyond our own".

Instead of giving a lead, the SMC had effectively retreated into a club for old codgers and actively shunned the new men. Murray and

Sid **Cross** (1913–1998) & Alice **Nelson** (1911–)

Sid Cross leading – note the rope loop runner

Alice Nelson, known to her friends as 'Jammy'

Among the working-class climbers of the 1930s, two of the most impressive were Sid Cross and Alice Nelson, a couple of young Kendalians who formed a skilled and formidable climbing partnership. Unlike many Lakes-based climbers of this time, who tended to restrict themselves to particular mountain ranges or valleys, they ranged widely over the district, bicycling to Langdale and then walking over the mountain passes to camp.

Their fitness and energy is exemplified by the way they tackled the severe winter route *Steep Gill* in 1938. This is the most difficult and serious of the traditional Lakeland gully climbs, with sparse protection on the crux section and unthinkable consequences in the event of a fall. Nevertheless the pair recalled the climb as 'fun' and in fact have more to say about the tricky descent from an iced-up *Broad Stand*, which Alice actually jumped down, such was her confidence. The reason for the hurry was the need to get down to Langdale before nightfall, in order to cycle back to Kendal that evening to be ready for work the next morning. Walking 20km, ascending 910m, climbing a serious Grade V route, followed by cycling 30km would be a pretty tough test for any modern triathlete, but to do it for fun and making it in for work at K Shoes at 8 a.m. the next day suggest exceptional levels of fitness, competence and enthusiasm.

In the latter part of the '30s they continued to undertake serious winter routes up to Grade V in both the Lakes and Scotland. Their record is especially significant in two ways. Firstly, they regained, then surpassed, the technical heights that had been achieved in winter, then lost through the Great War. Secondly, the co-equal rôle of a woman is remarkable on routes of this difficulty during the late '30s; Alice Nelson was almost certainly the first woman in the world to climb Grade V. Even today, women operating at this level are comparatively few in number, emphasising how far ahead of the times Nelson was in terms of attitude and ability. Given that she was just as adept on pure rock – she was the first woman to lead Scafell's inter-war test-piece route *Central Buttress* in 1939 – Nelson might arguably be described as the best all-round British female mountaineer of the inter-war years.

In 1949 the Crosses (Sid and Alice married in 1939) took over Langdale's *Old Dungeon Ghyll* hotel. Here, they created the famous climbers' bar which became one of the key base camps from which the explosion of post-war energy and talent was unleashed. Sid and Alice became unofficial guardians to gangs of unkempt and impecunious climbers, among them such luminaries as the young Don Whillans and Joe Brown. It was also during this period that Sid became instrumental in setting up what was to become the Langdale Mountain Rescue team, and, resourceful as ever, developed advanced rescue techniques, pioneering the use of dogs to locate casualties in the Lakeland mountains.

Eiger Nordwand (3,970m)

other youngsters had to set up their own networks and clubs, such as the Junior Mountaineering Club of Scotland.

This situation contrasted markedly with the senior club in the Lake District, the Fell & Rock, which was far less exclusive. Not only was it unique among the climbing clubs instituted before the Great War in admitting membership to either sex right from its inception in 1907 (the SMC would not allow women members for a further three-quarters of a century), it also encouraged working-class youngsters to join. There were thus crucial differences between the Scottish and Lake District climbing scenes; differences which led to a more rapid resurgence of climbing in England and Wales, and to English climbers gaining the initiative in pushing the technical standards in both summer and winter. This fact would be highlighted when Lakes-based activists later made sporadic raids to the north; Lakeland climber A.T. (Albert) Hargreaves's 1933 route *Rubicon Wall*, for example, remained the hardest summer climb on Ben Nevis until 1940.

'I doubt if there were then climbers in Scotland able to lead it in the middle-thirties', thought Murray. Nevertheless, despite effectively having to start climbing from first principles, big breakthroughs were made by Murray and his young Scottish friends, especially in the realm of winter climbing. Most Friday nights through the hard winters of the 1930s would see a small band of enthusiasts battling through the snowdrifts of Glencoe to engage in mammoth bouts of step-cutting using specialised shortened ice picks up icy gullies or spindrifted ridges. Although they didn't realise it, they were inventing a unique style of winter climbing and the technology to go with it, which was far in

advance of anything practiced anywhere else on snow and ice. They laid the foundations for their post-war Scottish successors to make the hardest ice routes in the world in the ensuing decade.

Munich Crisis (1936)

In a remarkable parallel to the general political scene, British climbing was becoming more insular, keeping a wary eye on distasteful continental practices, but choosing to ignore them in the hope that they would go away. When British climbers did deign to cast their eyes abroad, it was usually drawn to the romance and lure of the Greater Ranges situated in, or close to the borders of, Empire territory. Because of this, many climbers in Britain were unaware of the radically different line of evolution that continental climbing had followed.

In Britain, the emphasis was still firmly placed on clean climbing: ascending a route from top to bottom with no artificial aid in the form of metal pegs (*pitons*) driven into the rocks. Pitons were barely tolerated for protecting the climber either (in other words, threading the rope through a metal link in the peg to help arrest any fall). By common consent, all protection used in Britain was ideally natural, using what features came to hand by chance (such as rope slings placed over rock spikes, or the rope threaded behind a chockstone jammed into a crack).

Although this led to an ethically very pure and environmentally-friendly style of climbing, it did mean that the absolute technical limits of difficulty could only be achieved at considerable risk to the lead climber. Indeed, it makes the

British inter-war domestic climbing all the more outstanding. But it also meant that the technical limits reached were necessarily lower than could be physically achieved using artificial means of protection, or as help to overcome extreme passages of rock.

Few such qualms were felt on the continent where the sheer scale of many of the cliffs and mountains, and the danger from loose rock and weather encouraged, from the late-20s onwards, the use of every aid the climbers could get their hands on. Intense nationalist competition between Alpine climbers from Germany, Italy, Switzerland and France to climb the outstanding lines also helped to blur ethical considerations, especially when it was fuelled by an intense media interest virtually absent from the British scene. This sometimes led to long ladders of pegs being driven into cliffs in an attempt to subdue fearsome climbs.

During the 1930s the competition crystallised around the quest to climb the major Alpine north faces, or *Nordwands*, and as it intensified, climbers became almost reckless, as exemplified by the horrific attrition suffered by (mainly German and Austrian) teams attempting the notorious *Eiger Nordwand*. Team after team flung themselves at the notorious face under the full view of the tourist telescopes at Kleine Scheidegg, only to suffer horrible deaths or injury at the hands of rockfall or storms. French alpinist Armand Charlet summed up the atmosphere for many:

'This is not climbing, this is war.'

Colin **Kirkus** (1910–1940)

Away from his fusty, mundane job as a Liverpool clerk, Kirkus escaped into an alternative life as a futuristic cragsman. He specialised in steep, committing climbing at a time when protection was rudimentary and few thought it prudent. An enviable natural ability and confidence enabled him to play a significant rôle in opening up the forbidding verticalities of *Clogwyn Du'r Arddu* (it is Kirkus who is credited with coining its colloquial moniker 'Cloggy') and he undertook the first climbs on Scafell's bulging, barrelling *East Buttress*.

In the early 1930s he was clearly one of the UK's best climbers and had high hopes of being selected to join the 1933 Everest expedition. He was to be disappointed. The socially-exclusive predilections of the Mount Everest Committee were given voice by expedition leader Hugh Ruttledge: 'I am coming more and more to the opinion that we must beware of the north British school of rock-climbers if we are to succeed on Everest. Individually they are probably good men, but they are a very close corporation, with, it seems to me, a contempt for every one outside their own clan.' Up against prejudices like this, a civilian Scouser like Kirkus, without a university education, stood little chance.

Instead he went to the Indian Himalaya where he undertook a brilliant and futuristic alpine-style ascent of **Bagirathi III** (6,454m). Following this high point, Kirkus's enthusiasm for hard climbing was stymied in 1934 when an accident on Ben Nevis injured him and killed his partner Maurice Linnell. Nevertheless, clear signs of a recovery were apparent by the late 1930s when Kirkus's infectious enthusiasm for the sport was translated into one of the most engaging instruction books ever written, *Let's Go Climbing!*

Sadly, he was killed shortly afterwards, shot down over Germany on a wartime bombing mission.

The evolution of climbing equipment

Right: Alice Nelson's climbing boots

Rock climbing

By modern standards, the margins of safety within which '20s and '30s climbers were operating were still very small. But climbers were now much more sophisticated in protecting themselves from being pulled from the rock after George Abraham had first outlined the principles of secure belays.

A.B. (Alan) Hargreaves epitomised the new spirit; 'A belay to him is an engineering problem,' wrote his friend Colin Kirkus, 'He delights in constructing safe anchorages in the most appalling situations.'

Equipment, however, had scarcely changed from that employed before the Great War. Nailed boots were still the weapon of choice for the feet, although now shod with specialised replaceable soft metal nails called tricounis. Climbs of

considerable difficulty and sophistication were regularly achieved with such apparently unwieldy footwear.

Nevertheless, for the very hardest climbs on dry days, a pair of plimsolls was preferred by the majority. Plimsolls or 'rubbers' had been used before the Great War but there had been some resistance to them as cheating and 'not giving the rock a chance'. However, on the much harder routes of the '30 they came into their own.

Ropes had increased in length from 18m to 24m or even 30m but they were still rather inelastic and heavy and prone to break rather easily during falls.

Winter climbing

Climbers like Sid Cross and A.T. (Albert) Hargreaves manufactured much of their own kit, such as waterproof overmitts constructed from the rubberised canvas used in soft-top cars. Old waxed jackets cast-off from wealthier folk were re-proofed, cut down to waist level, and served as robust waterproofs. Underneath the trousers, pyjama bottoms were worn, much as thermal leggings are today.

Nailed boots were still *de rigeur* for winter climbing. Crampons had been around since classical times, but Oscar Eckenstein designed a pair of 10-point crampons in the early 1900s – a development of Victorian 'climbing irons'. They were heavy (nearly 1kg) and their use in Britain was frowned upon. Instead the nail was king.

In the Lake District it was no ordinary nail – the *Hargreaves Nail* was an innovative screw-in toothed metal plate, specially designed to be attached to the sole of the boot with two screws (Inter-war climbers used to carry screwdrivers to tighten loose nails). The Hargreaves Nail seems to have been more or less restricted to the Lakes, where A.T. had them made

specially at a bloomery in Ulverston, a dozen costing around 1/- (5p); very reasonable compared with commercially-derived tricounis at between 3/- and 9/- (15p–45p) a dozen. Its use undoubtedly contributed to the success of the Lakeland climbers of this time.

Above: Alice's boots showing the Hargreaves Nails

In winter, long 36m ropes were used, which gave a considerable advantage for the extended run-outs typical of winter, but to balance the extra weight there was a switch from full-weight hemp to thinner, one-inch (2.5cm)circumference line.

Long-handled ice-axes were still the order of the day for most climbs, but for harder ascents a shorter tool was necessary. In a remarkable example of convergent technical evolution, both Sid Cross and Albert Hargreaves in the Lake District, and Bill Murray in Scotland, first tried cutting the long handles off their axes. When this proved unsatisfactory, due to the unbalanced nature of the shortened axe, they independently adapted industrial tools for use on steep snow and ice; in Murray's case a slater's pick, Cross and Hargreaves an entrenching tool. Climbs would be tackled, as today, with two ice tools. The long axe would be for the approach and general ice-work, the short tool for cutting in confined spaces or steep ground where it was less tiring and cumbersome to swing.

Renny Croft and Tim Noble on *Mickledore Grooves* (VS 4c) on the *East Buttress* of **Scafell**

German climbing had been particularly afflicted by jingoistic nationalist fervour, encouraged by the Nazi Party and, although far from being restricted to that city, the new extreme form of no-holds-barred climbing became known as the 'Munich School'. Although their style was widely reviled by the British ('Conquest is only effected by the means employed by steeple-jacks when dealing with factory chimneys', thundered Colonel Strutt, editor of the *Alpine Journal* 'a repulsive farce which could only bring discredit on mountaineering'), the familiarity of the new breed of continental climbers with extreme ground had given them the confidence to tackle some extraordinary routes. It meant that the highest standards in Europe were considerably more advanced than much of British climbing – a fact most British climbers were complacently unaware of.

The visit of a group of Bavarian climbers to Britain in 1936 as guests of the Worker's Travel Association highlighted the philosophical differences that had developed between the British climbing scene and that of the continent. The Germans immediately impressed their British hosts by easily climbing some of the Welsh test-pieces in wet conditions in their specialised rope-soled *kletterschuhe*, which offered superior performance to the nailed boot.

But as the visit progressed, with continuing rain, they appalled the British by starting to place pitons for protection. Things came to a head when the Germans put up a new, hard route on the historic climbing ground of the Welsh mountain **Tryfan** (917m) They placed three pitons in the course of the climb, outraging the establishment and provoking the talented British climber John Menlove Edwards to repeat the route without using the pegs – which were removed shortly afterwards.

The Munich climbers moved on to further controversy in the Lake District where they placed further pitons on the hallowed Scafell route, *Central Buttress*, brilliantly climbed under appallingly wet and slimy conditions. After just a fortnight, the Germans left for home, leaving behind them a fulminating British establishment, smugly condemning the 'Munich Tactics'. However, the controversy served to hide the sizeable superiority in technical climbing ability, which the Germans had displayed, and it was also partly disingenuous. Pitons had already started appearing on British cliffs, placed by British climbers in increasing numbers, albeit reluctantly and only on the hardest routes. Although the British were loath to admit it, they were going to have to adopt some of the continental European tactics if their climbing was to advance.

On the eve of the Second World War, however, the philosophical differences between British climbing and the continent remained as wide as the English Channel.

Andy Kirkpatrick aid climbing on *Zenyatta Mondatta* (A4), El Capitan, Yosemite National Park, California.

Aid (Artificial) Climbing

As ever more difficult and steep rock faces were tackled during the early part of the twentieth century, some continental climbers sought to overcome 'impossible' passages using aids such as metal pegs (*pitons*) driven into cracks for direct pulls, with loops of rope attached for the feet (*étriers*). Techniques had become very sophisticated by the 1920s, though there was great resistance to them in the UK, where they were dubbed 'Munich Tactics' and 'Mechanised Climbing'.

After the war, the approach became more acceptable in the UK, and most of the hardest climbs were achieved with a few points of aid. The ethical standards were still very strict, exemplified by the self-imposed rule of Joe Brown, *the* most prolific leading climber of the '50s, who famously rationed himself to no more than two pegs per pitch of difficult climbing. During the 1960s almost completely artificial climbs were undertaken on some extremely overhanging cliffs. The training-led revolution in climbers' strength, stamina and fitness during the '70s led to a great culling of aid points and the majority of British routes are now free-climbed. Specialised aid climbing techniques are still used extensively on overseas Big Walls, however, such as the huge blank granite faces of the Yosemite Valley in the US.

Climbing Everest 8

(1933–1953)

I sometimes thought that bedsores were a more serious hazard than frostbite or strained hearts.

Mount Everest (8,850m)

Eric Shipton, 1933

Glace ceiling
The frustrating '30s (1933–38)

After the shock of the disappearance of Mallory and Irvine, no further expeditions to Everest were launched for nine years. This was not out of a feeling of respect, (although there was certainly plenty of that), but rather because the touchy Tibetan Government had become increasingly irritated by the repeated incursions into their still-secretive society by large parties of Europeans. Their ire had been especially raised after 1924 thanks to the antics of John Noel, the expedition's official filmmaker. On the 1922 expedition Noel had dragged his enormous cameras to 7,000m, where he stayed for a fortnight, setting an altitude endurance record and shooting over 3,000m of film under dreadful conditions.

Back in Britain, the film met a reception of uncomprehending indifference from a public yet to be exposed to the documentary format. Many complained about a lack of love interest and snowy base camp scenes of bearded men smoking pipes failed to excite a sense of wonder. Nevertheless, the film made a small profit and ran for 10 weeks at London's Philharmonic Hall. Because of this, it was thought worth repeating the exercise for the follow-up expedition in 1924 and, once again, the co-opted *auteur* Captain Noel was put back in the director's chair. Thanks to the sensation generated by the deaths of Mallory and Irvine, Noel's second film was an overnight success. But the canny Captain was taking no chances and decided to liven up proceedings by bringing a troupe of Tibetan Lamas to England to perform religious rituals and dance before each performance. This incensed the Dalai Lama so much he banned further expeditions in a fit of pique, and the Brits were kept out for 9 years.

Resumption of battle
The 1933 expedition

By 1933 relations had calmed and after considerable diplomatic pressure, the Tibetans reluctantly gave permission for a renewed attempt at climbing the peak. The 1933 expedition was led by Hugh Ruttledge, an India Office civil servant who, although well-travelled in the Himalaya, was not experienced in technically-difficult climbing. The appointment of Ruttledge, along with a team that comprised elements of the British Indian Army establishment and Cambridge University mountaineers, would lead to divisive tensions on both the 1933 and 1936 Everest expeditions. On both expeditions, the more ambitious mountaineers felt they were being held back by the excessive caution of the leadership.

In terms of equipment, the 1930s expeditions had hardly progressed since the Victorian era. Single-skin nailed leather boots were still *de rigeur*, and in the freezing temperatures of high altitude, invariably had to be thawed over candle flames so that the climbers could get their feet into them, bulging as they were with five pairs of socks. Each climber was kitted out in two pairs of long woollen pants, and wore seven Shetland wool sweaters, with a hooded windproof over the top. Shipton recalls that:

> *"I felt about as suitably equipped for delicate rock climbing as a fully rigged deep-sea diver for dancing the tango."*

Despite the personality clashes and the inadequate clothing, the British climbers once again proved that the two things they did not lack were courage and persistence. The two lead climbers, Frank Smythe and Eric Shipton, rapidly hewed a ladder of steps in the ice to the *North Col*, fixing ropes and ladders so that the rest of the expedition and their porters could follow and supply the advancing camps. From this position, they constructed a series of camps leading up the long ridge towards the summit.

The first of a series of major disagreements between expedition members occurred over the siting of the crucial Camp V at 7,620m, from which the summit attempts would be launched. Birnie, one of the military climbers, called off the advance at only 7,315m on the grounds that

Opposite: The monastery at Rongbuk. It has become traditional to seek the blessing of the Head Lama before the assault on the mountain

Captain John Noel and his 'bloody cinema'

he considered the Sherpas were exhausted, much to the annoyance and disgust of Cambridge climber Percy Wyn-Harris. On their return to the *North Col* there was an outburst from Wyn-Harris. Ruttledge had to read him the riot act regarding discipline, but displayed Solomon-like wisdom by immediately putting him in charge of the next attempt to place the high camp.

Pressed by the news from the new-fangled radio apparatus that the monsoon appeared to be arriving early in the Bay of Bengal, Wyn-Harris and fellow Cambridge climber Lawrence Wager made the first summit attempt, following the line taken by Norton on his record climb in 1924. They were turned back by treacherous new snow on the now infamous 'sloping tiles' geology of the upper section of the mountain, but not before they had made the startling discovery of an ice-axe. The axe must have belonged to either Mallory or Irvine and its discovery helped to re-ignite the debate over their predecessors' fate. Shipton and Smythe came up next to the high camp to have a go at the summit but were immediately pinned down for two days by a ferocious storm. On the third day, the weather cleared and they staggered out of their frozen tent without bottled oxygen and tackled the fearsome shelving rock band, relying solely on the insecure friction from their bootnails on the slippery, sloping surface. Shipton had to turn back due to sickness, leaving Smythe to forge ahead solo. Smythe reached 8,573m – an altitude that many pre-war climbers seemed unable to exceed – before he decided it was wise to retreat in the face of deep new snow. The arrival of the full-blown monsoon meant the end of the expedition and yet another defeat at the hands of Everest's fickle weather.

Surprised by events
The 1935 reconnaissance expedition

The 1935–6 Everest expeditions were a surprise to everyone – the Mount Everest Committee included. After the 1933 expedition, Britain's Political Officer in Sikkim reported: 'The Tibetan Government did not want any more expeditions at all because they caused offence to the gods and trouble to the country'. So when the 13th Dalai Lama died and there was a devastating earthquake in neighbouring Nepal, chances of permission appeared slim, but amazingly the Tibetans gave the go-ahead.

The Committee was understandably unprepared. Things were further complicated by the fact that attempts were being made to change the old-fashioned *status quo* favoured by the selection panel, with its heavy emphasis on social background and contacts. In the words of Shipton's biographer, Peter Steele: 'Battle lines were drawn between the Old Guard, imperial explorer-proconsuls, and the rude, brash, ribald younger generation of top climbers'. Much argument and bad feeling was generated before there was a slew of outraged resignations from the Committee and an inevitable compromise. Ruttledge, the non-mountaineer 'whom everyone liked but nobody wanted' remained overall leader, but control of climbing decisions fell to leading climbers Frank Smythe and Eric Shipton.

In the meantime, before a full-scale expedition could be mounted, Shipton was despatched to Everest in 1935 on a reconnaissance trip to observe the behaviour of snow conditions during the monsoon period – a practical matter about which very little was known. He was further charged to spy out the unknown *West Ridge*, but not to enter forbidden Nepal in which it

Frank **Smythe**
(1900–1949)

Frank Smythe wasn't the first person to exploit the commercial possibilities of writing about his mountaineering exploits, but he was the first to make it into a successful business. His output was prolific (comprising 27 books in 20 years and dozens of articles) and his influence is discernible on the format of photographic mountain books to this day. His mountaineering travelogues have inspired numerous imitators. His reputation amongst his peers suffered from overexposure in the popular media of the day, however, exemplified by Raymond Greene's exquisite put-down, 'Physically on mountains, intellectually in his books, Frank always tried to reach heights which were just a little beyond his powers, great though these were.'

Smythe was more than just a self-publicist however; his literary and photographic ability alone would have come to nought had he not accomplished many fine ascents in the Alps, (particularly with T. Graham Brown on Mont Blanc) as well as playing a central rôle in inter-war high-altitude mountaineering. His many Himalayan expeditions included attempts on **Kangchenjunga** (8,586m) in 1930, climbing the highest peak then attained – **Kamet** (7,756m) – in 1931, as well as the three 1930s Everest expeditions. Arguably his finest hour involved his alpine-style climbs in the Indian Garhwal in 1937.

All this was achieved despite an allegedly frail health and physique (Smythe, who was deemed unfit for strenuous sport at school, only embarked on his astonishing climbing career after being invalided out of the RAF in 1927).

His solo bid for the summit of Everest in 1933, when he reached a high point of 8,573m without bottled oxygen has been described as 'the most notable performance until Reinhold Messner made his solo ascent nearly fifty years later.'

He died attempting to resume his Himalayan career in 1949 when he was taken ill in India.

was situated, so he was able to peer into the *Western Cwm*. Although no one yet realised it, this would be the route which would eventually prove to be the key to the mountain.

In his favoured lightweight and highly mobile style, Shipton contrived to accomplish all the objectives set him, *and* climb 26 peaks. 'About as many peaks of over 20,000ft (6,090m) were climbed in the Himalaya as have been climbed since the days of Adam', marvelled climbing veteran Tom Longstaff.

The following year, yet another full-blown, lavishly-resourced expedition set forth to attempt the peak. Shipton was reluctant to go, after tasting the freedom of his smaller expeditions, but felt compelled to comply thanks to professional pressures – in common with his fellow lead climber Frank Smythe, he had no other major source of income than writing about his climbing activities.

'A thorough washout'
The 1936 attempt

The 1936 Expedition lumbered forward through Tibet in time-honoured manner via the Rong-buk Monastery where it received the now traditional blessing from the Head Lama. Sadly, this was to have little beneficial effect. As so often in the 1930s, the monsoon arrived early and snow began piling up in huge drifts on the mountain shortly after the team's arrival at base camp. Although dogged journeys were made up to the *North Col*, conditions were terrible and Ruttledge recalled everyone from the mountain.

But before total abandonment, Shipton and Wyn-Harris made a final trip up the mountain to verify that conditions really were hopeless,

more out of frustration than real hope. This was definitively confirmed when Shipton set off an avalanche which carried him down towards a sheer drop. Wyn-Harris managed to jump off the conveyor belt of sliding snow and dig the shaft of his ice-axe into the lip of a crevasse and hold Shipton on the rope.

The expedition beat a retreat with its tail between its legs. Once more, the weather had defeated dogged persistence.

'A vile waste of time'
The 1938 lightweight expedition

The fifth abortive attempt to climb the mountain took a radically different approach to all its predecessors. Influenced by the remarkable success of Bill Tilman's lightweight Nanda Devi expedition, the Everest Committee invited him to apply a similar approach to climbing the world's biggest hill. But, they were not only influenced by ethical considerations: the Committee was almost broke and the prospect of an expedition costing only a fraction of previous attempts was highly attractive. Newspaper sponsorship was harder to get because of the history of failure but the lack of publicity suited Tilman, who hated the razzmatazz and attendant lack of privacy of commercially-funded expeditions.

The team of seven (which included Shipton and Smythe) were all climbers – there were to be no supernumeraries on this trip. The team's departure from the British Isles was also refreshingly low-key compared with previous expeditions: instead of brass bands, popping flashbulbs and cheering crowds, only Tom Longstaff and Shipton's girlfriend were there to wave them off at the station.

To everyone's disappointment, the weather was vile once more, with an exceptionally early monsoon. The expedition battled up to the *North Col*, in spite of horrendously deep snow and made a gallant attempt on the summit before admitting defeat. Even so, Tilman had demonstrated that a small, determined team could get as high on the mountain as any large expedition; a lesson which was largely ignored for the next 30 years.

Unlocking the key
The 1951 Everest reconnaissance

The exploration of Everest was interrupted by the Second World War and its aftermath. When it did resume, the political map had changed radically with significant ramifications for the style and geographical approach taken.

Tibet had been invaded and occupied by Communist Chinese forces in 1950, effectively barring the traditional northern approach used by all expeditions thus far. In contrast, Nepal, which had remained politically isolated for centuries, began to open up and the British were unexpectedly granted permission to approach Everest from the south. Taking advantage of this unprecedented change of policy, the newly convened Mount Everest Committee sent Eric Shipton on a reconnaissance expedition in 1951 to assess the feasibility of this approach. Shipton established beyond doubt that a practical route lay up the mountain from this direction, although it did necessitate entering the treacherous and unpredictable Khumbu Icefall, a dangerous cataract of tumbling glacier that regularly shed huge blocks of ice. Nevertheless, this was to prove to be the key to climbing the mountain.

The Swiss give the Brits a fright
(1951–2)

Another thing had changed in the post-war world: the demise of the British Empire. In the years leading up to the war, Everest had rather been assumed to be a British preserve – it bore a British name, it was near to British territory and had been attempted almost solely by British climbers.

This nationalistic 'colonisation' of prestigious Himalayan Peaks was not confined to the British: the Germans famously considered **Nanga Parbat** (8,125m) 'their' mountain, the French became enamoured with **Annapurna** (8,091m), while the Italians and Americans became fixated with **K2** (8,611m).

The fact that Everest was the highest peak in the world meant it was unrealistic that climbers from other countries would not soon take an interest when the old 'special relationship' of the British with Asia began to break down in the post-Imperial era. Nevertheless it came as a shock to many in Britain that this was the case, and when the Swiss came close to success on the peak in 1952, it caused consternation in the Joint Himalyan Committee (as the revamped Mount Everest Committee was now known). Hillary summed up the unspoken feeling:

> *"It was strange how we resented this news;*
> *as though Everest belonged to us and*
> *no-one else had any right to it."*

The British had permission from the Nepalese to try the mountain in 1953, but should they fail, French and Swiss teams were lining up to have a go. A feeling close to high anxiety appeared to have gripped the decision-makers in London. In their eyes there was more than climbing a mountain at stake, national prestige depended on it. In a series of political manoeuvrings, they ousted the popular, but laid-back and romantic civilian Eric Shipton from leadership of the 1953 expedition, and replaced him with a thruster; the no-nonsense logistics expert Colonel John Hunt. The last chance to plant the Union Flag on the highest point on the Earth had been felt to be too important to leave to an amateur. 'We've got this one chance, and if we don't get it right we've had it. And dammit, it's our mountain', the Himalayan Committee's secretary told Hunt. The old-fashioned amateur approach had been decisively squashed by a new sense of corporate management. Shipton was devastated by the harshness of his treatment, as were most of his team, many of whom offered to resign in support, but he urged them to lend full support to the new leader.

Left: Climbers beneath the *Lhotse Face* of Everest

'All this and Everest too!'

The New Elizabethans triumph at last (1953)

Right: Tenzing Norgay and Mike Westmacott examine the tents to be used on the Everest expedition

To quote climbing commentator Jim Perrin, 'the 1953 venture was less expedition and more expeditionary force'.

The British were determined not to fail this time and, for once, everything seemed to go in their favour. The weather was reasonable, John Hunt's revered organisational ability lived up to expectations, the team was a strong and happy one and, arguably most importantly, they had got the science right. At long last, efficient compact oxygen apparatus was available. Dr Griffith Pugh, a physiologist, had studied the requirements carefully on previous expeditions and was the expedition's expert on the oxygen apparatus. Had worked at the General Medical Council on the physiological effects of extreme environments. Michael Ward went so far as to say:

"Pugh was the only indispensable person… if he had not done his research we would not have climbed Everest in 1953."

Members of the triumphant 1953 British and Commonwealth Everest Expedition – *from left:* Alfred Gregory, Michael Ward, Tom Stobart, George Lowe, Griffith Pugh, Edmund Hillary, John Hunt, Wilfrid Noyce, Tom Bourdillon, Tenzing Norgay, Charles Evans, Mike Westmacott and Charles Wylie

The sum of all these factors led to the moment sought by so many climbers for so long: the summit.

On 29th May New Zealander Edmund Hillary and Nepalese Tenzing Norgay Sherpa 'knocked the bastard off' (in the colourful language of the earthy Hillary). Neither was actually British, but it seemed like it at the time. The news was rushed back to Britain just in time to coincide with the coronation of the new Queen Elizabeth on 2nd June. The country, still burdened with post-war rationing and austerity measures, went mad with pride. 'All this and Everest too!' gushed the *Daily Express* headlines.

Everest was climbed, a country rejoiced. To many in the mountaineering world, it seemed that an era had come to an end, that one of the last great secrets had been revealed. To some, this was not necessarily a bad thing. Eric Shipton fervently hoped that having exorcised that particular demon, the limelight might shift from mountaineers and they could get on with exploratory climbing on smaller peaks without the pressure of being flag-bearers for national prestige.

This was to prove far from the case; the apogee of nationalism in Himalayan climbing was just beginning as the competition to climb all the 8,000m peaks intensified. Everest continued, and continues, to exercise a powerful hold on climbers' imaginations. Five decades on, the mountain is still rarely far from the headlines, although often for reasons less happy than its first ascent in 1953.

Ed Hillary having a welcome cuppa on arrival at Camp VI – in Tom Stobart's mug!

Left: Edmund Hillary's photograph of Tenzing Norgay Sherpa taken at 8,850m on the summit of Mount Everest on 29th May, 1953

Above: While still not to be taken lightly, nowadays it is possible to join a commercially-guided expedition to **Everest**. Here, preparation is under way to leave the *South Col*

Sir Edmund **Hillary**
(1919–)

It was perhaps inevitable that one the first people to clamber atop the planet's biggest mountain would turn out to be a larger than life character himself. Edmund Percival Hillary, a bold, brash, bombastic beekeeper from New Zealand had already had a more eventful career than most before the climactic events surrounding his moment of triumph on Everest with Tenzing Norgay Sherpa.

A redneck upbringing in New Zealand led to adventures in the Southern Alps, where Hillary learned the craft of ice-climbing. It was while on a shoestring Kiwi expedition to the Indian Garhwal in 1951 that he cheekily hitched aboard the British Everest reconnaissance expedition, led by the famously laid-back Eric Shipton. Impressed by Hillary's sound mountain-craft and fortitude at altitude, Hillary was invited onto the following year's training expedition to **Cho Oyu** (8,201m) and the 1953 Everest attempt.

His infamous antipodean directness was exemplified by his frank appraisal of his achievement which he gave to George Lowe on the *South Col*. 'Well, George, we knocked the bastard off'. Presumably his language was slightly moderated when he received his knighthood from the Queen.

Although several mountaineering ventures followed his Everest triumph, Hillary ironically suffered from ever more severe bouts of altitude sickness, ensuring that his energies were increasingly channelled into adventures on the horizontal rather than the steeply inclined plane.

In 1956–8 he drove a converted farm tractor all the way to the South Pole – the first trans-Antarctic crossing – and has been involved in river-rafting expeditions and trekking ventures, before turning politician. Hillary has also been heavily involved in issues concerning the welfare of the Sherpas of Nepal, to whom he has devoted a lifetime of help with aid programmes.

The Cragrats

Post-war British climbing

(1945–1970)

I often wondered what the tourists thought of us. They would stare curiously at our tatty clothing and bulging 'sacks, but whenever you caught their eye, they looked quickly away. We didn't exist in the same world.

Don Whillans, archetypal '50s climbing 'Hard Man', taking the Montenvers train, French Alps, 1954

Left: Mick Burke under the *West Face* of the **Petit Dru** (3,730m) which overlooks Chamonix

69

The arrival of the flat hat (1945–1960)

Unlike the after-effects of the Great War, the post-1945 period saw a great increase in both the numbers participating in the sport and an improvement in the standards at which it was practiced. There are two main reasons for this.

Firstly, the climbing scene was not immune to the socio-economic changes resulting from the war, which affected all aspects of society. Economic recovery during the 1950s and rising prosperity thanks to rising employment levels were allied to the more egalitarian ethos prevalent in post-war Britain. A new generation of working-class youngsters found themselves with a modest amount of disposable income and there was a gradual increase in mobility as petrol rationing began to relax, allowing more traffic onto the roads, which in turn helped climbers reach their destinations by hitch-hiking. As time went on many climbers invested in motorcycles, opening up more areas for week-end climbing.

Secondly, equipment began to improve. Climbing had been commandeered during the war as a method of training crack assault troops. Because getting up things quickly was their main aim, rather than an ethically admirable ascent, anything went, including grappling irons, pitons, slings and metal snaplinks, or karabiners. Large amounts of this specialist equipment was manufactured, along with more general protective clothing. The cessation of hostilities allowed such ex-military kit to become available at low cost.

Above: Alpine campsite in the '50s during the preparations for a big climb

Climbers were able to improvise suitable climbing gear from the anoraks, rubber-cleated boots and rucksacks. More importantly, nylon slings and steel karabiners were also widely available for the first time. These could be used to thread the climber's rope quickly through protection and were important in increasing the safety of the lead climber. Grappling irons were left in the bargain bins.

The result was that a sport which had hitherto been overwhelmingly the preserve of the middle- and upper-middle-classes was subjected to an invasion of plumbers, chippies, welders, and any number of other tradesmen. This explosion of untapped climbing talent, for

so long suppressed in the industrial cities, spilled out of the urban centres next to the hills of northern England, Wales and Scotland and onto the crags. These new climbers were generally fitter, stronger and tougher than their predecessors. They climbed more regularly, and also persevered longer when conditions were bad, rather than waste the effort and expense of a precious weekend of free time just because it was lashing down with rain and freezing cold.

Typical of the new breed were two plumbers from Manchester, Joe Brown and Don Whillans. Both men were from humble inner-city backgrounds, brought up in the backstreets of Manchester's Rusholme district and Salford. Both, like so many ground-breaking climbers before them, had served a climbing apprenticeship on the short, severe outcrops of *Millstone Grit*. They formed a partnership during the 1950s which forged new climbs of much greater difficulty than had been normal before. Brown possessed a natural poise and balance, Whillans a forceful, muscular style. Together they greatly advanced British climbing, producing climbs which were revered as the epitome of difficulty for a decade or more, and which are still respected today.

Brown's 1951 ascent of *Cenotaph Corner*, for example (a plumb-straight crack soaring up the centrefold of the great open book corner of *Dinas Cromlech*, an imposing cliff in Snowdonia's Llanberis Pass), was both a technical and psychological breakthrough. Unremittingly steep, the climb required the leader to undertake technical and strenuous climbing many feet above protection for sustained periods. To climb it, he had to be both good and strong – and have a cool head.

Whillans produced routes of similar magnitude both in partnership with Brown and with others. Their legacy of climbs epitomises this fabulously creative era of British rock climbing. Both Brown and Whillans were associated with Manchester-based Rock & Ice, the club which included many other fine climbers. The routes put up by this élite grouping attracted an aura and kudos which would hold for most of the decade, before general levels of fitness and boldness began to catch up with the leaders.

The Brown/Whillans partnership led to a resurgence of climbing in this country, resulting in British climbers coming back into contention in the Alpine arena. In 1954 they made the third ascent of the then cutting-edge route, the *West Face* of the **Petit Dru** (3,730m), a soaring orange spire of granite towering over the glaciers above Chamonix. They not only climbed the route, but also completed it in a very fast time and in doing so became the first British climbers to compete on equal terms with top continental alpinists since the Great War. Remarkably, they were achieving impressive ascents like this while operating on a shoe-string budget. The contrast between the impecunious Britons and the sophisticated continental climbers they were competing with, was emphasised by Brown's memory of the day after their historic climb:

"Louis Lachenal, one of France's foremost guides, came to pay his respects. He was dressed immaculately and was escorted by a gorgeous girl. He found the party lounging on the ground in filth and squalor, like a band of brigands. Goodness knows what he thought of us."

Opposite: Rusty Baillie on *Cenotaph Corner*, first climbed by Joe Brown in 1951

the Baron

Joe **Brown** (1930–)

Joe Brown is rightly revered among rock-climbers. At his peak he had a mastery of technique and balance that was way ahead of his time – in the 1950s there was arguably no finer climber in Britain. Along with Don Whillans and others, the former plumber and property repairer helped to propel rock climbing to new heights of difficulty during the post-war decades.

Brown's climbing skill was multi-faceted; he excelled in the Alpine arena too, and became one of the world's leading mountaineers when he climbed the third-highest mountain in the world, **Kangchenjunga** (8,586m), with George Band in 1955. In the 1960s and '70s Brown continued to innovate, opening up previously undeveloped climbing areas in the UK such as the sea cliffs of Anglesey and continuing his mountaineering exploits in places as far flung as South America, Russia and Pakistan.

Brown's influence over the sport was given a wider currency in the '60s by his frequent appearances in early TV outside broadcast spectaculars. From the mid-'60s to the mid-'70s, Brown was almost as prominent a media personality as Chris Bonington, being invariably described by the tabloid moniker 'The Human Fly', as he stuck to precipitous cliffs for the camera. But even without this media exposure, Brown is arguably *the* British climber of the twentieth century.

His skill and vision helped pave the way towards the modern concept of the sport, while his climbs continue to be among the most exciting, challenging and sought-after routes in the country.

the Villain

Don **Whillans**
(1933–1985)

In popular legend, Donald Desbrow Whillans always seemed to be wearing a flat hat and punching someone, usually a continental climber, whilst clutching a pint and riding a motorbike. This caricature assumed the dimensions of a kind of Mancunian Popeye, but with more wit and a beer belly.

Whillans started on this road to comic deification with his cutting-edge partnership with 'Human Fly', Joe Brown in the '50s, although in Whillans's case 'fly' always seemed a bit too insubstantial. The climbing 'brick' might have been more appropriate.

The combination was awesome: Brown with his eye for a classic line and levitational ability, and Whillans with his mighty strength and toughness. Together they rewrote the rulebook of British climbing, powering up steep, scary lines in the Peak and Wales which had been regarded as impossible by the pre-war generation of climbers. Whillans blazed a trail for the British revival in the Alps too, climbing with a range of partners and making many significant ascents including the first ascent of the difficult *Central Pillar of Frêney* with Chris Bonington in 1961.

By the mid '60s Whillans was becoming more interested in expedition climbing – and socialising, as his increasing girth began to testify. Arguably his greatest mountaineering moment arrived on the summit of **Annapurna** (8,091m) in 1970 when, with Dougal Haston, he battled up an extremely arduous rock and ice wall on the mountain's *South Face* against all the odds.

Whillans also brought to bear a strength of character to match his physical prowess; in his encounters with officialdom and other climbers he rarely came off worse. As a result a working-class macho reputation preceded him wherever he went, making him perhaps the most popular climbers' icon of the 20th century. His wit and predilection for a pint made for many memorable one-liners, delivered with his distinctive nasal Salford tones:

Why do you drink so much Don?
'Aye, well I've got this morbid fear of dehydration.'

When do you stop drinking before going on an expedition Don?
'When I reach the last pub'.

Sadly, Don died of a heart attack in 1985, but the fact that a generation of climbers is still recounting Whillans's anecdotes is as fine an epitaph as his legacy of climbs.

Winters *of* content

Scotland takes the lead in ice climbing

(1950s)

Vicious weather conditions and technical severity mean that Scottish ice climbing is always a challenge, even with modern equipment

A similar class revolution had taken place in Scottish rock climbing in the post-war period, with members of the working-class Creagh Dhu Club, such as Clydebank shipyard worker John Cunningham, in the vanguard of putting up climbs of extreme difficulty on Scottish cliffs.

They were viewed with some trepidation by the established hierarchy represented by the Scottish Mountaineering Club. One member writing at the time, viewed the invasion of the hitherto privileged domain of the Highlands by the proletariat with bemusement:

"The new group of climbers find themselves not so much heirs to a tradition as discoverers of a secret kept hidden from their class."

As climbing writer Ken Wilson later wrote, 'It was rather as if a group of East-Enders had suddenly decided to take up grouse-shooting or polo'. Although the new climbers, who were stronger, fitter and tougher, were to play the game harder and better, they still abided by its unwritten rules: there was to be no wholesale importation of continental-style ethics. New climbers also began to push the standards in Scottish winter climbing, although the leading players tended to be from a more traditional middle-class background, albeit mediated by the socialising influence of the post-war university system.

Thus, in the Cairngorms, Aberdonian medical student Tom Patey began exploring the huge mixed snow, ice and rock buttresses, while on Ben Nevis ex-public schoolboy and philosophy student Robin Smith teamed up with the older Edinburgh architect Jimmy Marshall to embark on a series of ice climbs which were the hardest in the world. By 1960 the pair had established a peerless collection of major ice routes such as the alpine-scale *Orion Face Direct*. Routes such as this would be regarded as so advanced that they would not be repeated for well over a decade, and then only when technology had changed the nature of ice-climbing such that it was less tiring and committing than hacking holds out of the ice with a single ice-axe.

Above: *'Trust me, I'm a doctor!'*
Dr Patey puts a new design of
mountaineering helmet to the test;
Chris Bonington is the willing guinea pig

Tom **Patey**
(1932–1970)

Aberdonian Tom Patey remains one of Britain's great climbing icons whose lustre has scarcely diminished since his premature death in 1970 at the age of 38. This is somewhat ironic, given the fact that Dr Patey, a practicing GP, was one of the most iconoclastic characters to grace the anarchic post-war scene. Patey was celebrated during the '50s and '60s as one of the greatest amateur climbers, pioneering new routes in both winter and summer in many places (including the Karakoram), but primarily in the Scottish Highlands.

The popular doctor is widely credited with reviving interest in the Cairngorms in the '50s, opening everyone's eyes to the potential of the north-west Highlands and, despite suffering from the finger-numbing Raynaud's Syndrome, making breakthrough post-war winter climbs and starting the trend towards mixed winter climbing that would lead to its burgeoning popularity in the '80s and '90s. Even though these achievements would have been sufficient to ensure his place in the climbing hall of fame, they were complemented by his multi-talented abilities as a satirist, humourous essayist, raconteur and, accompanied by his trusty accordion, general all-round pub entertainer. He was, quite simply, a song-and-dance-and-rock-and-ice-man *sans pareil* – and consequently extremely popular amongst his peers. British audiences were particularly enamoured of Patey's self-deprecation and refusal to take anyone or anything terribly seriously. That he managed to signal his identification with climbing's counter-culture without alienating the British climbing establishment is a measure of the charm and charisma which he possessed.

One of Patey's later passions was climbing remote, wave-washed sea stacks off the Scottish coastline and it was during an abseil descent of one of these that he fell to his death in 1970.

The **rock** *and* **roll years**
(1960–1970)

The 1960s were to see further changes in the social structure of the climbing community. The expansion of the higher education system meant that students and university mountaineering clubs began playing an important part in the development of rock climbing.

The end of national service in 1960 liberated many into the arms of these institutions where, thanks to long holidays and the student grant system, young climbers enjoyed a lifestyle less constrained by penury or social convention than their working-class predecessors.

There was also an expansion of the professionalisation of climbing as more and more local authorities began following the lead of Derbyshire Education Committee and opened Outdoor Education Centres. They joined the other private outdoor pursuits centres, such as those of the Outward Bound movement. These had been set up after the war following the educational principles of Gordonstoun founder, Kurt Hahn, who advocated mountaineering and small boat sailing as character-building experiences for youngsters. These establishments not only created the possibility, for the first time, of a career structure for professional climbing instructors, but also introduced thousands of schoolchildren to the sport, many of

The **evolution** of **climbing equipment**

3

During the mid-1950s, the French climber, Pierre Allain, had developed a specialised tight-fitting rubber-randed rock shoe which permitted much more use to be made of small delicate footholds. The 'PA', as it came to be generically known, was quickly adopted by the élite climbers and came into virtually universal use by the 1960s.

At the same time, much stronger slings and ropes became available making the sport safer. Another safety development that found favour during the '50s was the use of small pebbles, which were jammed into cracks in the rocks behind which slings could be threaded. The leader's rope was then clipped onto this with a karabiner, providing a running belay in the event of a fall. During the 1960s the concept was refined and adapted by threading line slings through industrial nuts, which could be placed in cracks directly. The idea caught on rapidly, multiplying the protection possibilities enormously and increasing the safety of many routes immeasurably. The industrial nuts were soon replaced by specialist metal wedges manufactured in a variety of sizes specifically for climbing.

Another development of great significance was the invention of the climbing harness. From the beginning of the sport the rope had been simply tied around the waist of the climber. When a fall occurred this was very uncomfortable and the sudden constriction as the climber's weight came on the rope could even cause injury. A climber could also only hang in free space for a relatively short period of time before the pressure

Above: Early nuts

would render him unconscious. The appearance of the sit-harness, manufactured from nylon webbing made falling safer and much less uncomfortable. It also provided somewhere to hang all the new metal chocks and nuts that '60s climbers began carrying.

whom would go on to swell the ranks of recreational climbers.

All this was set against a background of ever-increasing climbing standards. By the end of the decade a great many average rock-climbers were regularly operating at the 'Very Severe' level of climbing difficulty, a grade which had been regarded as still quite respectably hard at its beginning. New areas were being opened up in addition to the traditional mountain and outcrop centres. Sea cliffs, such as those of Anglesey and Cornwall were being explored and disused quarries were being climbed in geographical locations without any previous history of climbing activity. The traditional territorial boundaries of climbers were breaking down for good as car ownership soared and information became easier to obtain. It no longer mattered where you lived in the country, it was possible to climb regularly either on local outcrops or within comfortable travelling distance.

However, top climbers were reaching a kind of physical limit. Climbing was still undertaken very much in an amateur spirit and training was not taken seriously. Instead the climbing community generally adhered to a collective ethos of anarchy; many regarded the pub and the party as an acceptable preparation for a day on the crags. As a result, climbers sought to open up unclimbed areas of rock using a bit of help.

The 1960s saw a proliferation of artificial aid pitches appearing on the hardest new climbs.

The use of pitons, of course, had been regarded almost as a sacrilegious act in Britain before the war, but now it was becoming more acceptable to use direct pulls on them to overcome short sections of rock which appeared to be unclimbable by free methods. This was still not without its critics, but as long as the number of aid points was kept down to a minimum, it was tolerated as a legitimate way of breaching new ground. The sight of a peg hammer dangling from the waist of a corduroy-breech-clad climber as he strolled to the cliffs with his nylon rope coiled over his shoulder marked him out as one of the 'Hard Men'. For this was still very much a macho sport.

There were certainly women climbers out there, and even female mountain guides such as Gwen Moffat, but they still formed a minority of participants and, outside the sisterhood of the Pinnacle Club, an all-female rope remained a rare sight.

However, all this was about to change as the '60s became the '70s. Revolutionary changes in equipment and attitudes towards the sport were to transform climbing standards across the board and increase the demographic profile of participation yet again.

Television
& climbing

Public exposure to climbing increased in the media throughout the 1960s. The first climbing magazines in the modern sense began to appear regularly, but the most significant publicity was through a series of television outside broadcast spectaculars of rock-climbs which appeared regularly through the 1960s. The first of these took place on *Clogwyn Du'r Arddu* on Snowdon and proved so popular with the viewing public that further events were staged around the country, most famously on Orkney's spectacular sea-stack *The Old Man of Hoy*.

Above: BBC Live Outside Broadcast – *Old Man of Hoy*, Orkney Islands, 1967. Rusty Baillie *(left)* and John Cleare prepare their broadcast equipment for the climb. Both men also carry the usual climbing and safety gear – they must each climb carrying over 22kg

Above: On 14th July 1965, a combined BBC and Swiss Broadcasting project broadcast live television pictures of the ascent of the Matterhorn 100 years – to the very hour – after the first ascent of the Matterhorn by Whymper's party, as part of the celebration of the Year of the Alps

Left: Pictures from the summit of the Matterhorn. Ian McNaught-Davis, the BBC climber/commentator *(right)* interviews Heinrich Taugwalder, great grandson and grandson of Old and Young Peter Taugwalder – guides on the first ascent. Climber/cameraman Hamish MacInnes operates a BBC radio camera in the foreground

From Himalayan Circus *to* Alpine Style

(1955–)

For a mountaineer, surely a Bonington Everest expedition is one of the last great Imperial experiences life can offer.

Peter Boardman, 1975

Left: Shishapangma (8,027m), one of the world's 14 8,000m peaks

Upward mobility
(1955–1975)

The British and Commonwealth Everest Expedition of 1953 was significant in more ways than one. With the battle to climb Everest finally won, British climbing was released from a kind of national obsession which had begun half a century earlier. British climbers started looking elsewhere in the Greater Ranges, towards other great 8,000m prizes and lesser peaks. But the '53 expedition also marked the passing of another era. In many ways it was the Last Huzzah of the old establishment way of recruiting climbers for prestigious mountaineering expeditions. From now on, the class distinctions of the pre-war decades would begin to count for less and the composition of an expedition would increasingly be planned along meritocratic lines.

By the mid-1950s the same democratising spirit which had changed the demographic profile of the domestic rock-climbing scene began to influence mountaineering in the Greater Ranges. Ordinary people began to be invited on expeditions – but only if they happened to be extraordinary climbers. In this way the 'climbing plumber', Joe Brown, was invited to join the 1955 expedition to the world's third-highest peak, **Kangchenjunga** (8,586m). The successful conclusion of the venture (Brown summiting with George Band, the youngest member of the '53 Everest team) announced the arrival of the post-war climbing generation in the Greater Ranges.

It was only a matter of time before the new wave of climbers began attempting their own campaigns in the Greater Ranges without waiting for an invitation. One of the earliest and most audacious of these was the Creagh Dhu Everest Expedition of 1953. The 'expedition' was made up of just two climbers, only one of whom, John Cunningham, was actually a member of the famous Glasgow climbing club. His partner (and instigator of the venture) was Hamish MacInnes: a climber of legendary resourcefulness who possessed a mind attuned to solving mountaineering problems with a unique brand of lateral thinking.

MacInnes had recognised that the unsuccessful 1952 Swiss expedition to Everest must have left behind a huge supply of unused food, oxygen and equipment, including tents. Therefore, why bother raising a huge expedition from scratch as the English were doing, MacInnes reasoned, when a couple of Scots could storm the Khumbu Icefall and make use of all that *in situ* quality Swiss infrastructure?

Cunningham had personal worries about his lack of high-altitude experience. Such doubts were swept aside by the boundless confidence of his partner. 'Well, you've done Ben Nevis,' MacInnes argued, 'so the next logical step is Everest.'

With the force of this impeccable logic to steady them, Cunningham and MacInnes set forth carrying the entire expedition supplies on their backs in two 65kg rucksacks. Meanwhile the British and Commonwealth Everest Expedition of 10 climbers, 34 Sherpas and 300 porters was already in Kathmandu. It was an unequal contest of course and the big guns beat the cocksure Scots to the summit. Nevertheless, the fact that the shoestring tartan team not only managed to get to Everest base camp, but succeeded in ascending an unclimbed 5,950m rock spire, spoke volumes for the latent ambition and drive existing amongst the climbing masses. Confident 'can-do' attitudes like theirs signalled that the mould of the privileged pre-war expeditions had been broken and that from now on, climbers from all social backgrounds would also participate in tackling the big mountains.

By the end of the 1950s, nearly all the 8,000m peaks had been climbed. As happened in the Alps a century earlier, interest switched from gaining the summits by the easiest line to attempting more difficult routes to the top. Most expeditions continued to follow the traditional pattern used during the first part of the twentieth century in adopting so-called siege

Hamish MacInnes – all of the supplies for his Creagh Dhu Everest Expedition with John Cunningham in 1953 were carried in two 65kg rucksacks

Chris Bonington using the solar-powered Apple IIc computer that he took all the way to Camp II on his 1975 conquest of Everest. Bonington, formerly a proponent of siege tactics, has since gone on to lead much more streamlined expeditions

tactics. Consecutively higher camps would be established on the mountain, supplied and serviced by support climbers and porters, until the expedition was in a position to send acclimatised lead climbers to the top camp and, hopefully, the summit. This approach involved large numbers of people, equipment and time, and was invariably very expensive. It also often led to fixed rope and other detritus being left on the mountain.

The advantage of this approach was that it offered a systematic and flexible way of tackling the problems inherent in climbing the huge 7,000m+ peaks of the Himalaya. In addition, although the big mountains were, by their very nature, always going to be very dangerous, siege tactics offered at least the prospect of prepared escape routes, sliding down fixed ropes to high camps if retreat proved necessary. The large numbers of people involved also held out the possibility of rescue for climbers in difficulty, although in such difficult terrain, this was usually more of a comforting illusion than a real prospect.

The disadvantage was that many climbers found the experience of being part of a large regimented team, with sometimes little individual chance of getting to the summit, to be an alienating one. It seemed a far cry from the liberating sense of freedom that drew them into climbing in the first place. The more jaundiced amongst the disillusioned dubbed the whole experience a 'Himalayan Circus'. Nevertheless, the conventional wisdom until the mid-1970s was that large expeditions were the only way you could realistically hope to climb the very highest mountains.

Everest the hard way
(1972–1975)

The scale of expeditions reached new heights in the early 1970s when, once again, the magnetic attraction of Everest drew the most ambitious climbers back to the Khumbu. After the summit had been climbed by the easiest route, it was only a matter of time before the other facets of the mountain came under attack from ambitious climbers. The *South-West Face* of Everest was an obvious target.

Chris Bonington had been thinking about this objective for some time. During the late '50s and early '60s, Bonington built up an impressive portfolio of mountaineering achievements. Through much of the '60s he was also involved in pursuing a career in photojournalism, but in 1970 he returned to élite mountaineering and masterminded the ascent of the *South Face* of **Annapurna** (8,091m) in Nepal.

This triumph was significant on two counts. It marked the start of a new era of Himalayan climbing – never had such a huge, steep face been climbed at such altitudes. Furthermore, the summit (eventually gained by the oldest member of the team, the redoubtable Don Whillans, and one of the youngest, charismatic Scottish climber Dougal Haston), was attained without the use of supplementary oxygen. More prosaically, it allowed Bonington to gain valuable expertise in organising expeditions – and also in raising the funding to support them from sometimes surprising sources.

To tackle a face this large using traditional siege tactics required a vast amount of equipment, people and money and Bonington used all his charm and communication skills to raise money from business and the media. The

marketing of prestigious mountaineering ventures on this scale and the degree of commercial sponsorship required was unprecedented. Bonington's approach generated some controversy – but its efficacy was undeniable.

His success on Annapurna set the pattern for equally ambitious, high-profile attempts on the *South-West Face* of Everest in 1972 and 1975. Four other major siege-style expeditions had attempted this side of Everest before, and Bonington's initial 1972 attempt joined them in failing to surmount this huge and difficult face.

Undeterred, he planned to return for another attempt, but mountaineering pundits gave him no more than a 1 in 7 chance of success. Bonington's 1975 expedition, however, confounded his critics and was a resounding triumph, albeit marred by the death of climbing cameraman Mick Burke. Following the technically demanding climb, which had required a high level of teamwork, the successful British summiteers, Dougal Haston, Doug Scott and Peter Boardman, became household names. The stature and seriousness of the achievement is emphasised by the fact that the *South-West Face* has since been the subject of only three repeat ascents (one of which resulted in the deaths of the four summiting climbers).

Everest 'The Hard Way' as it became known, consolidated Bonington's position as the world's most successful expedition organiser. He had not only planned and orchestrated the logistical complexities of the expedition with the then novel aid of a computer, but he had persuaded Barclays to bankroll the expedition to the tune of £100,000 – no mean feat in the midst of national economic turmoil resulting from the oil crisis of the early '70s. He also promoted the achievement so successfully, that the title of the expedition book resulted in a new phrase being coined – the habit of appending 'the hard way' to any sentence where difficulty needed to be emphasised appears to date from this time. Despite its success, however, the sheer scale of the set-piece expedition juggernaut seemed to have been almost too much for all the climbers involved to bear. ('For a mountaineer, surely a Bonington Everest Expedition is one of the last great Imperial experiences life can offer,' Boardman had commented ironically, boggling at the huge caravan of porters and support staff during the approach march). The expedition therefore marked a kind of watershed in British mountaineering. From then on, leading mountaineers, Bonington included, accepted that they were philosophically inclined towards much smaller-scale, less environmentally-damaging mountaineering, which allowed a more intimate and individually-fulfilling experience for the climber. The question was: could such an approach be adopted on the highest peaks? The main protagonists of Everest '75 were to play a major rôle in answering that question and, in the process, help to swing cutting-edge mountaineering towards a new era of super-alpinism.

Back to basics
Alpine style returns (1975–)

The concept of attempting to climb the highest mountains in much the same way as one would approach an alpine ascent – starting from the bottom and carrying all your equipment with you up to the top and back down again – was not a new one of course. One of the first attempts to climb a Himalayan peak, that of A.F. Mummery in 1895 on **Nanga Parbat**

(8,125m), had been alpine style and had reached 7,000m. Colin Kirkus and Charles Warren had also pointed towards the future with their magnificent lightweight ascent of the Garhwal peak **Bagirathi III** (6,454m) in 1933 and, of course, the over-riding preference of the great Shipton and Tilman was for a simplified approach. Nevertheless, the ideal was rarely acted upon until the mid-1970s, when a series of bold alpine-style ascents by various European climbers began to demonstrate what was possible.

White Van Man hits the Himalaya
Tasker & Renshaw on Dunagiri (1975)

An influential British ascent of this period came in 1975 when two relatively unknown British climbers, Joe Tasker and Dick Renshaw, climbed the *South-East Ridge* of **Dunagiri** (7,066m) in the Indian Garhwal. The story of their trans-continental journey from Manchester to the Himalaya in a tatty Ford Escort van was almost as monumental as the ground-breaking climb itself, involving as it did crossing the ruts and chaos of Iran, Afghanistan and India, but the ascent itself was immediately recognised as outstanding.

Not only was the expedition extremely compact (two people!) but the climbing was extremely demanding. They ran out of fuel and food on the descent and were pushed to extreme physical limits, Renshaw suffering frostbite to his fingers and both climbers completely exhausted by the time they got down. The climb showed, however, that a very small team of climbers could tackle technically difficult Himalayan peaks without recourse to vast armies of porters or bottomless budgets.

Joe Tasker (1948–1982) & Pete Boardman (1950–1982)

Joe Tasker *(left)* and Pete Boardman on the 1982 British Everest Expedition – sadly their last

Boardman became famous in 1975 when he summited **Everest** (8,850m) as only the third Briton. Despite this success, Boardman felt he had to prove something to his peers and launched himself at the distinctly futuristic *West Wall* of Changabang with Tasker the following year. The big differences in personality (Boardman the diffident, well-spoken English Lit. graduate, Tasker the intense abrasive craftsman), did not prevent the partnership becoming triumphant and the pattern was set for a whole series of expeditions to the high places of the earth, including **K2** (8,611m), **Kangchenjunga** (8,586m) and **Mount Kongur** (7,719m) in China. The pace was hectic and the risks high. In 1982 the pair disappeared attempting the highly technical *North East Ridge* of Everest.

In addition to their climbs, the pair left a legacy of extremely influential books which showcased an exceptional literary ability to match their mountaineering prowess. Appropriately, the annual *Boardman Tasker Memorial Award for Mountain Literature* is named in their honour.

Joe Tasker tried many careers before becoming a climber. Starting off as a Jesuit seminarian, he was at various times, a dustbin-man, quarryman and sociologist before he finally plumped for a life of alpine adventure. Tasker followed a prolonged alpine apprenticeship, often climbing with Dick Renshaw, specialising in insecure mixed faces. Together they made the long-awaited first British winter ascent of the *North Face* of the **Eiger** (3,970m) and followed it up with an audacious two-person ascent of the highly technical **Dunagiri** (7,066m) in the Indian Himalaya, travelling all the way to their destination in a £170 Escort van.

Tasker teamed up with Pete Boardman shortly afterwards to push the standards of technical rock climbing at altitude on **Changabang** (6,866m) in the Indian Garhwal and thence entered the spiral of constant expeditioning.

On **Kangchenjunga**

Left: Changabang (6,866m)

The trend was set, and other highly-influential British alpine-style or semi-alpine-style ascents followed, such as Tasker's and Boardman's two-man ascent of the fearsomely difficult granite *West Wall* of **Changabang** (6,866m) and the 1977 ascent of **Jannu** (7,710m) by young British climbers Alan Rouse, Brian Hall, Roger Baxter-Jones and Rab Carrington.

Such alpine-style ascents meant, of course, climbing without the aid of bottled oxygen, something which required extremely good acclimatisation and fitness.

A further spur to the advocates of alpine style at this time came from the remarkable oxygenless 3-day dash up the 8,068m **Hidden Peak** by the Tyroleans Reinhold Messner and Peter Habeler. Nevertheless, there remained very real doubts in many climbers' minds that it would be possible to survive, let alone climb, at such rarefied heights. Messner and Habeler quashed that notion completely when they climbed Everest in the same way in 1978 and when Messner followed up his achievement with a solo of the mountain without oxygen in 1980. It became obvious that given the right fitness, physiology and drive, no peak on earth was immune to the concept of the rapid, lightweight ascent.

It was arguably the alpine-style ascent of a difficult new route on Kangchenjunga in 1979 by British climbers Doug Scott and, once again, Peter Boardman and Joe Tasker, that proved the feasibility of small scale assaults on large scale objectives. In 1978, the Austrians had taken their training regime to obsessive lengths and been backed up by a support team using oxygen (although Messner eschewed the use of oxygen for his 1980 solo ascent), leading many to assume that, although possible, only well-financed supermen could carry off such feats. Not only was Kangchenjunga '79 the first time that one of the world's three highest peaks was climbed by a small team without others present using oxygen, but the climbers involved were far from being physiological freaks.

Alpine style rapidly acquired the status of orthodox faith for any aspiring mountaineer wishing to perform at the highest levels on the biggest mountains. The ideal is perhaps exemplified by Alex MacIntyre's ascent of the then unclimbed *South-West Face* of the giant Tibetan peak **Shishapangma** (8,027m) in May 1982 with Doug Scott and Roger Baxter-Jones. MacIntyre, along with virtually all the other prominent young alpinists of the late '70s, was a fierce advocate of the lightweight approach. It was symptomatic of a general reaction to the huge, sluggish, top-heavy siege mentality of the past 50 years. MacIntyre famously said of their ascent:

> *"The face was the ambition;*
> *the style became the obsession."*

This obsession led them to the foot of the 2,500m face. Without any prior knowledge of the ground ahead they started up it carrying four days' worth of food, a stove, sleeping bags and a tent and very little else apart from climbing equipment. Three days later they reached the summit and were back at base camp a day after that.

However like much else in climbing, alpine style is not a prescriptive term, with precise boundaries and rules. It is more of a general aim to attempt to do more with less. So there are sub-alpine style approaches, such as the so-called 'capsule' ascent, adopted where fixing short sections of rope may be preferable so that a return to a comfortable camp can enable a better rest before a final, true alpine-style push to the top. This was the approach taken on Boardman's and Tasker's 1976 *West Wall* of Changabang climb. The precise mix of approaches is irrelevant; instead the alpine-style ideal is usually considered to have been attained if the climb is achieved with a small self-contained team that has minimal environmental impact. The approach, although far more satisfying to the individual climber than the enormous siege expeditions of the past is, of course, highly risky. Small teams out on a limb have only their own resources to fall back on if the weather turns bad or if an accident should occur.

Above: Shishapangma (8,027m) seen from the Friendship Highway

Sir **Christian** John Storey **Bonington**, CBE
(1934–)

By far and away the most famous mountaineer in Britain, Chris Bonington has arguably been the public face of climbing for over three decades.

Born in Hampstead, Bonington went on to the Royal Military Academy at Sandhurst after public school and was commissioned into the Royal Tank Regiment in 1956. He concluded his military career as an instructor at the Army's Aberystwyth Outward Bound School.

Behind this official activity Bonington had begun carving a reputation as a forceful rock and ice climber in Britain, making the first ascents of difficult winter climbs in Glencoe and hard rock climbs on the limestone cliffs of the Avon Gorge. It was also during this period that Bonington began climbing in the Alps, making the first British ascent of the *South West Pillar* of the **Dru** (3,754m) with Don Whillans, Paul Ross and Hamish MacInnes in 1958. He followed this with the first ascent of the *Central Pillar of Frêney* (with Don Whillans, Ian Clough and Polish climber Jan Dlugosz) in 1961.

Bonington also accomplished the long-awaited first British ascent of the *North Face* of the **Eiger** (3,970m) in 1962 with Clough, thereby confirming himself as one the country's premier mountaineers. His first Himalayan venture was in 1960 when he reached the summit of **Annapurna II** (7,937m), followed by the *South Face* of **Nuptse** (7,841m) in 1961. This latter expedition, consisting of a small Manchester-based team, was well ahead of its time and arguably the first technical Himalayan face to be climbed using the primitive equipment of the time.

By now Bonington had left the army to become a management trainee at Unilever but, faced with the choice between selling margarine and a life of adventure, he chose the latter. In 1963 he climbed in Patagonia, succeeded on the difficult granite spire of the **Central Tower of Paine** (2,799m) with Don Whillans. This was to be Bonington's last climbing expedition for seven years as he developed his career as an adventure journalist. He returned to the fray in 1970, masterminding the groundbreaking ascent of the huge *South Face* of Annapurna – at 3,567m the biggest rock wall yet climbed in the Himalaya.

His success on Annapurna set the pattern for equally ambitious attempts on the *South-West Face* of Everest. He failed in '72, but his 1975 expedition was a resounding success, albeit marred by the death of cameraman Mick Burke. Everest 'The Hard Way' as it became dubbed, consolidated Bonington's position as the world's foremost mountaineering logistician, but he returned to his roots, embarking on a series of lightweight expeditions that he continues to pursue to this day.

Among the highlights of these later ventures is his 1977 first ascent of the fearsome 7,285m Karakoram peak **Baintha Brakk**, also known as *The Ogre* with Doug Scott, (which involved a nightmare retreat after Scott broke both legs and Bonington several ribs). In 1981 he led a team to the top of the remote Chinese peak **Kongur** (7,719m). In 1985 he finally reached the summit of Everest, a mountain which he knew so well but had never actually climbed. In between there have been numerous climbing trips around the world, to Greenland, Antarctica, the Caucasus, the Karakoram and Himalaya.

Despite this bulging climbing CV, Bonington has also found time to write numerous books, script TV documentaries, undertake exhaustive public-speaking tours, serve on numerous official committees – and even hunt for the Yeti! Although now eligible for a bus pass, there seems little chance of Sir Chris (he was knighted in 1996) hanging up his climbing boots just yet. He continues to rock-climb to a high standard (he recently pioneered new rock climbs in Morocco), and spent last winter climbing difficult snow and ice in Scotland, while the autumn of 2001 is set aside to explore the remote Ladakhi mountains of Arganglas.

Triumph & tragedy

Tales from the edge of endurance

A good example of the penalties some-times inflicted on lightweight teams occurred in 1977 on the Karakoram peak of **Baintha Brakk** (7,285m), more popularly known as *The Ogre*.

Right: The magnificent *West Ridge* of **The Ogre** on a clear day

Far right: That same ridge during the storm that hampered the descent of the injured Doug Scott, seen here crawling down to the top of the pillar

In 1977, a six-strong British team attempted the unclimbed mountain. The final, highly-difficult rock climbing section was blitzed by Doug Scott and Chris Bonington, Scott leading all the way up steep granite cracks and overhangs which, as he later recalled, comprised 'the hardest climbing I've ever done at altitude'. This simple comment gives a measure of the difficulty of the route – it came from one of the best mountaineers in the world.

They reached the summit at sunset without tents or sleeping bags and hurried to descend, fearful of the prospect of an enforced bivouac at altitude. While abseiling down, Scott skidded on some icy rock and swung into a gully wall, breaking both of his legs. The pair survived a freezing night on a tiny snow patch, massaging each others' toes in an attempt to ward off frostbite. The following day the nightmare retreat continued as they managed to reach the top snow-hole they had dug on the way up.

Here they were pinned down by storm, but were forced to move after two days before they lost all their strength. Helped by Mo Anthoine and Clive Rowland, who were waiting for them at the snow-hole, Scott hauled his way down on his knees (wearing out the knees of five pairs of overtrousers in the process). At one point a tired Scott abseiled right off the ropes but managed to save himself by instinctively grabbing the end of it in a reflex action. Bonington made the same mistake and broke several ribs, but his misfortune did not end there, as he developed pneumonia on the way down. They finally got back to base camp after eight days of agony. It had been a close-run thing, with disaster only just averted by the tremendous efforts of all the team to effect a self-rescue.

With emphatic understatement, Scott said afterwards of his ordeal:

> *"It was a severe lesson which I was lucky to survive and am not anxious to repeat."*

The Ogre still awaits a subsequent ascent despite twenty attempts.

Chris Bonington at base camp recovering from broken ribs and pneumonia

Doug Scott at base camp with both legs broken and abrasions on his knees after his epic on **The Ogre**

Doug **Scott** (1941–)

After Chris Bonington, Doug Scott is probably Britain's best known mountaineer, thanks to a 48-year climbing career that spans the globe and everything from small outcrops to 8,000m peaks.

Nottingham-born Scott first came to the fore in the British climbing world as an exponent of artificial climbing, tackling outrageously overhanging pieces of rock in Derbyshire and on outlandish cliffs in the Hebrides and Anglesey. He put his expertise to good use on the Big Walls of the Dolomites, Yosemite and Norway and, ultimately on Baffin Island in the Arctic.

Since the late 1960s Scott has become best known as a mountaineer, making first ascents and pioneering new routes on mountains in the Alps, Himalaya, Karakoram, Hindu Kush, Africa, Alaska, Canada, Russia, Arabia, Antarctica and Iceland. Scott first came to wide public prominence with his 1975 ascent of the *South-West Face* of **Everest** (8,850m) when he and Dougal Haston became the first Britons to stand atop the highest summit on the planet. Even more remarkably, they survived an enforced bivouac at 8,760m unscathed.

Scott's own predilection is for unobtrusive small-scale alpine-style expeditions, a passion he has spent most of the last 25 years pursuing. Amongst his myriad climbing ventures, some of the more influential have included his 1977 *tour de force* on **Baintha Brakk** (7,285m), also known as *The Ogre* (which involved the hardest technical rock climbing then achieved at high altitude and an epic descent with two broken legs) and

his alpine-style success on the third-highest mountain in the world, **Kangchenjunga** (8,586m), in 1979. This was the first time that one of the three highest peaks was climbed by a small team without others present using oxygen and it spurred others on to emulate the feat on the remaining 8,000m peaks.

A distinguishing feature of Scott's approach has been his concern for the mountain environment and the local inhabitants. He has been heavily involved in securing hygienic water supplies for villages in the Karakoram and Himalaya and runs a trekking business that prides itself on ethical treatment of its portering staff. Scott continues to chase ambitious new ascents in the Greater Ranges, having recently spent much time attempting new climbs on **Nanga Parbat** (8,125m) and is still passionate about climbing closer to home, despite nearly half a century of activity.

Shades *of* **Mallory** *&* **Irvine**
Tasker and Boardman on Everest

A happy ending such as that of the 1977 Ogre expedition was not in store for the ambitious lightweight attempt on the *North East Ridge* of Everest in 1982. This was by far the lightest attempt on that route, with a party of four climbers who intended to tackle a ridge sprouting fearsomely-difficult pinnacles high above 8,230m. If any team was likely to have succeeded on this most arduous of undertakings, it seemed that one comprising leading mountaineers Joe Tasker and Pete Boardman, along with Chris Bonington and Dick Renshaw was most likely to pull it off. In the event, Boardman and Tasker disappeared behind the pinnacles of the ridge, watched through a telescope by Bonington. They never reappeared. The attempt had been magnificent but had ultimately ended in tragedy – there were perhaps limits to what could be achieved using lightweight approaches. The route was finally climbed only after six further expeditions, all of which used a lot of fixed rope and Sherpa support.

Despite the fearsome risks, however, alpine style remains the dominant ethos which most ambitious British climbers strive to uphold. There are still many nations, particularly from Asia and the Far East, whose climbers retain a predilection for the heavyweight approach of fixed camps and fixed ropes. The growth of commercially-guided expeditions in the Himalaya and Karakoram has also perpetuated the siege tradition by professional climbers and their wealthy clients.

In parallel with this activity, however, the adventurous self-reliant approach has been carried to new heights and new places through the 1980s and into the '90s by climbers such as Mick Fowler and Victor Saunders, whose remarkable ascent of the Karakoram's difficult *Golden Pillar* of **Spantik** (7,027m) remains one of the most outstanding post-war British ascents. Recent successes, such as the 1997 ascent of the very difficult *North Face* of Changabang by Andy Cave, Brendan Murphy and Steve Sustad illustrate that committing, pure alpine-style ascents of technically-difficult mixed routes are still very much in vogue with the super-fit, even though they remain extremely risky, as shown by the death of Brendan Murphy on the descent.

Mick Fowler
(1956–)

'The *Mountaineers'*
Mountaineer'

Right: The *Golden Pillar* of Spantik (7,027m)

Inland Revenue officer Mick Fowler is an outstandingly gifted amateur climber, continuing a fine British tradition of modestly-understated adventures in the more remote mountains and cliffs of Britain and the world at large. His talent is such that he could probably have dominated any specific branch of his hobby, but instead he has bucked the modern trend towards specialisation and has packed more achievement into virtually every branch of traditional climbing than most pros can ever dream of.

His is a pioneering spirit, eschewing trends towards bolted climbing, to pursue lines up steep ice, crumbling chalk and shale, guano-stained sea-stacks and dangerous mountains. Fowler's new climbs can be found on rugged Scottish sea-stacks, fearsome Welsh icefalls, extreme gritstone outcrops, friable Devonian cliffs and remote, difficult peaks across the globe from the Americas to Russia and Asia. But Fowler is just as keen to pursue lines closer to home; he has even climbed a frozen outfall from a leaking gutter at St Pancras Station!

It was perhaps inevitable that when the *Observer Magazine* asked a range of leading British climbers to nominate their '*Mountaineers' Mountaineer*', it was the tax inspector from North London who came top of the *vox pops*.

Fowler's popularity with his peers does not stem from his climbing ability alone; he is renowned for his modesty and sense of humour. In an age of increasing commercial pressures, his outstanding amateur achievements remain an inspiration to many climbers.

Andy Kirkpatrick
in action

Dave Birkett bouldering
in South Africa

Dave Birkett climbing in South Africa

Andy Kirkpatrick committed on *Iron
Hawk*, El Capitan, Yosemite

Airlie Anderson on a Portaledge
belay in Yosemite National Park

Dave Birkett on Bleed In Hell (E7 6c)
Bowderstone Crag, Borrowdale, Cumbria

Ian Parnell jumaring, Pembroke, Wales

Modern Times

British climbing in the late 20th Century

$(1970-)$

The mental preparation was becoming harder
and harder. Gone was the initial naïvete which
had sparked off this terrifying enterprise.
I knew the score and was unnerved by it.

North Wales climber John Redhead
expressing doubts and fears inherent
in pioneering an 'Extreme' climb, 1980

The 1970–1985 period witnessed the most radical leap in standards of performance that climbing has ever experienced. Part of the reason for this was technological, part of it was down to training, and part of it was simply a shift in perception as to what constituted the actual limits of physical possibility.

Take your pick
Ice Revolution (1970–1975)

Unprecedented changes first became manifest in ice climbing. Until 1970, British winter climbing had scarcely changed since the Victorian pioneers had first hacked ladders of snow steps up the great couloirs of the Scottish Highlands. The method remained almost unendurably exhausting. Holds were fashioned for both hands and feet in the ice using an axe and the pitches free climbed. It was time-consuming, difficult and very, very cold. Although the adoption of crampons after the war had certainly improved security, and specially-shortened ice-axes made hold-cutting slightly less strenuous, it was still an incredibly tough way to climb. Accordingly, ice-climbing remained largely restricted to an élite body of (mainly Scottish) climbers. By the late '60s, this group had achieved some astonishingly difficult ascents, cutting their way strenuously up vertical hanging ice sheets, weaving across alpine-sized faces and spindrift-lashed buttresses, and conquering almost all the steep snow-packed gullies of note. After 1970, however, the way such routes were climbed was changed forever by new technology that opened up winter climbing to all climbers, not just those with bulging biceps and exceptional stamina. In that year Californian climber/engineer Yvon Chouinard marketed an ice-axe with a steeply curving pick which stuck firmly in ice, enabling the climber to make a direct pull up holding the shaft. This was revolutionary; traditional ice-axe picks were usually straight, and simply popped out when pulled. Using one of the new tools in each hand however, the climber could advance up steep ice rapidly, placing the axes securely, pulling up, removing a tool and re-inserting it higher like a portable hold. The feet could also be kicked into the ice without the need for cutting footholds thanks to forward-pointing spikes at the front of the latest design of crampons, which stuck in a similar way to the ice picks. This whole, somewhat mechanical, process was therefore christened 'Front-Pointing'.

Chouinard wasn't the only climber who had been thinking along these lines. The wily Glencoe-based Hamish MacInnes had also recognised the possibility of replacing step-cutting with direct pulls on ice picks. MacInnes had been experimenting with 'dropped' picks but had yet to hit on a satisfactory angle of droop. After meeting Chouinard in Glencoe in 1970, he suddenly realised the solution and produced a radically angled pick on a tool which would become the mainstay of British ice climbing for over a decade: the MacInnes *Terrordactyl*. (illiterately named after its supposed resemblance to the head of the famous flying dinosaur.)

Armed with the new tools, the hardest routes immediately became easier to climb. The results were dramatic. Climbing commentator Paul Nunn wrote that almost overnight…

> *"… generations of technique and mountaineering practice of considerable sophistication went out of the window, jettisoned like an old sock."*

The time taken to climb testing and revered routes like Ben Nevis's top grade *Point Five* and *Zero* gullies were more than halved by 1971; by 1973 both had been soloed in three hours by Scots climber Ian Nicholson.

Climbing with *Terrordactyls*

Ron Fawcett climbing *London Wall* (E5 6a), Millstone Edge, Derbyshire

Nevertheless, winter climbing was still a strenuous, sweaty business and remained a dangerous undertaking. Insecure belays were still insecure, and protection stayed illusory on many routes. Climbing ice may have become physically easier, but getting up to and off the climbs, dodging avalanches and avoiding poor weather remained as difficult as ever. Although the number of ice-climbers increased exponentially, it remained a junior cousin of rock climbing, at least in terms of participation. A further evolution in ice-tool technology was to occur in the 1980s when 'reverse curve' or 'banana' picks were introduced, which allowed even better performance. An unexpected bonus was the new tools' efficacy on snowed-up and ice-glazed rock. Experimentation by Scottish pioneers such as Murray Hamilton, Kenny Spence and Andy Nisbet showed that by twisting, or 'torqueing' the tools in cracks, strenuous progress could be made up very steep ground, even with only a thin snow cover. This discovery led to a second revolution in winter climbing, causing the proliferation of a new style of technically-hard mixed routes on previously impossible terrain which continues to this day.

Professional attitudes
Rock revolution (1970–1980)

The improvement in the standard of rock climbing during the 1970s was extraordinary. The difference in the difficulty of the hardest routes between the beginning and the end of the decade was probably greater than all the advances of the previous thirty years. As in ice climbing, technological development helped bring about the change, but there was also a

much more fundamental shift in the way top climbers approached the sport. For the first time, training for climbing began to be taken seriously. Several key personalities played a prominent rôle in bringing about this paradigm shift.

The first of these was a young student called John Syrett. When he arrived at Leeds University in 1968, Syrett had scarcely climbed before but, for some mysterious reason, felt drawn to the then state-of-the-art mountaineering wall at the university (which was little more than a brick wall with some bricks missing). Following 12 months of assiduous indoor training, he transferred his artificially-enhanced skills to Yorkshire outcrops in the summer of 1970, climbing many hard routes of the day, often solo, and pioneering lines of advanced difficulty. His ethical approach was greatly admired, and helped influence a change of attitude in the '60s climbing scene which was still heavily-dependent on artificial aid.

Keen observers of developments duly took note: amongst them an outdoor-education lecturer and part-time climber, Pete Livesey, who set to musing what wonders a sports plan might do for his own prospects. Like Syrett, Livesey decided to apply the obsessive training ethics of professional athletics to the hitherto happy-go-lucky, 'pub-trained' arena of rock climbing – and improved radically. During the first part of the decade, the rangy, iconoclastic Yorkshireman was climbing two grades harder than everyone else. It took a while for other top climbers to catch up. In the meantime, Livesey started popping up all over the country, from the Lakes to Cornwall, bagging previously unimaginable lines, removing the aid points from strenuous peg routes and out-climbing

Pete Livesey

the local experts. No corner of the country seemed safe from his raiding prowess for a while in the mid-70s, armed as he was with his seemingly bionic powers and a hit list of famous crags carefully designed to ensure maximum publicity. The Livesey phenomenon galvanised the British rock climbing scene and a new vitality was injected into the pioneering of new routes all over the country. For the rest of the decade rock climbing standards increased year by year and the elimination of aid on already-established lines (the so-called 'freeing' of routes) was pursued with almost religious zeal. The atmosphere of feeding frenzy was encouraged by the maturing of a domestic

The **evolution** of **climbing equipment**

1970s

During the 1970s, cutting edge climbers were helped in their quest for ever higher standards by enormous strides in climbing equipment. In 1976, Californian climber Ray Jardine invented a spring-loaded camming device that could be inserted in cracks in the rock and which could hold a falling climber when the rope was clipped through it. These 'Friends' as they were called, opened up protection possibilities in the most unlikely of places, including flaring cracks and helped boost the confidence of the lead climber.

At around the same time, improved wired metal chocks with tapered faces became generally available in a multitude of sizes, enabling still further running belay possibilities.

The improved protection meant that skillful climbers no longer felt constrained by the time-honoured maxim that 'The Leader Must Not Fall'. Instead, falling off became commonplace, as climbers strove to achieve moves close to the limits of their physical capability, with their confidence boosted by the knowledge that the risk of serious injury was much reduced.

Finally, an important addition to the armoury of high standard climbing was the introduction of gymnasts' 'chalk' (magnesium carbonate). This, like Jardine's camming devices, came into British climbing via sunny California where climbers had found that it greatly helped reduce the lubricating effects of sweat on fingers. Its validity in the thermally-challenged climate of the UK was doubted at first, and there was also considerable resistance on ethical and environmental grounds (although some climbers had experimented with resin in order

to make their fingers stickier as long ago as the '30s). However, chalk marks left on the rock face could give a clue to the direction of a line, thereby reducing the route-finding element of a subsequent ascent to a 'join the dots' exercise. The majority of climbers found chalk helped their performance on the harder routes, however, and Britain's wet climate meant that in most places the white dabs periodically disappeared. Even so, chalk use is rather habit-forming, which means that even beginners can be seen plastering the large holds of easy climbs with white dust where it can give no realistic help. Chalk remains one of the unresolved ethical dilemmas which have consistently plagued British climbing in recent years.

1980s

Technological advances continued improving the performance of climbers into the 1980s. At the beginning of the decade the design of rock-shoes had changed little from the original 'PA' design of the 1950s. Top rock-climbers would willingly cripple themselves by squeezing into shoes several sizes too small in order to increase their ability to stand on the tiniest of holds. In some cases, they tried rubbing resin onto the soles in order to increase the stickiness of the rubber.

In the early 1980s, however, such desperate measures were made unnecessary by the Spanish footwear manufacturer *Boreal* who introduced a rock shoe with a new sticky rubber-compound sole. It made an enormous difference on the hardest routes where matchstick-width holds or friction moves were critical to success and helped to fuel the increasing rise in the standard of the hardest rock climbs.

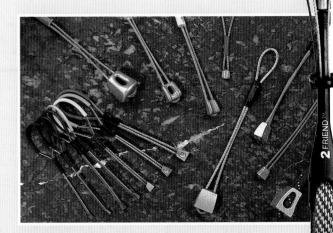

Other developments in rock climbing hardware that date from this period include: minute brazed RPs – brass nuts for very thin cracks – and nuts with curved faces that improve performance through a simple mechanical camming action

In winter climbing and mountaineering the invention of plastic boots also allowed for much improved performance. Previously climbers had used very heavy double-leather boots, but the new technology of plastic shell and alveolite inner boots was much warmer, lighter, completely waterproof and did not freeze under extreme conditions.

Plastic boots rapidly became the standard kit for mountaineers.

climbing media; several large circulation magazines promptly recorded the new routes, further fuelling an already competitive atmosphere.

Livesey's example laid the foundations for the careers of other climbers, the most prominent of whom was fellow Yorkshireman Ron Fawcett. Fawcett, a tall, genial man with exceptional natural ability, a monster reach and vast reserves of bottle, built on the achievements of his friend Livesey and raised top climbing standards even higher. Significantly, he became the pioneer of a new type of professional rock-climber, who earned a modest living from sponsorship by equipment manufacturers. This was a radical departure from established professional climbing models, such as instructing, or earning money from lecturing and writing about expeditions. Instead, the relationship was more akin to that of a tennis player with a racquet or soft drinks manufacturer in that Fawcett promoted hardware or clothing by simply being associated with that product, being photographed for magazines and testing new designs. Unlike mainstream sports stars however, Fawcett never made a fortune, but he did pioneer a trend which has expanded enormously within the sport and become lucrative for those with the right talent, looks and contacts.

The banner of professionalism was inevitably raised higher during the materialistic '80s. Jerry Moffatt was the first British rock gymnast to profit comfortably from his sport. A true master of all aspects of moving over stone, Moffatt excelled at everything from three-move boulder problems at the limit of possibility to hair-raising solos of high, hard routes in the mountains. He even captivated a home crowd when he won one of the world's first indoor grand prix climbing championships.

Moffatt's ruthless dedication, creative approach to training and infectious enthusiasm have led the way for a new generation of sponsored athletes, including Ben Moon, John Dunne, Airlie Anderson and Ian Vickers.

Bolts, boldness and brand management (1980–1990)

At the beginning of the 1980s, rock shoes improved out of all recognition, thanks to the introduction of radical new sticky rubber compounds. By the end of the decade, artificial climbing walls for training began to become much more sophisticated, using new plastic compounds to shape holds and simulate real rock features. As a result, the training regimes followed by the élite activists of the '70s began to percolate through to the general climbing population, ensuring a rise in standards of performance: the so-called 'grade drift'.

Another factor encouraging the inexorable rise in standards was the general economic situation of much of the decade. High youth-unemployment resulted in a group of talented 'dole climbers'. They were epitomised by Bolton climber Paul Pritchard, who spent his days on welfare, becoming ever more skilled on steep rock and helping develop important new climbing grounds that had scarcely been considered before, such as the huge abandoned slate quarries of Llanberis. Such people – and their employed counterparts – became drawn to climbing towns. Sheffield, with its proximity to a vast range and variety of outcrop climbing and central location, became the undisputed capital of British climbing, with a higher concentration of active climbers than anywhere

Jerry Moffatt, the popular hero of modern rock climbing soloing *l'Horla* (E1 5c) Curbar Edge, Derbyshire

Paul **Pritchard**
(1967–)

To many, the appearance on the climbing scene in the mid-80s of Bolton back-street boy Pritchard came as a breath of fresh air. Here was someone who appeared to be recapturing the romantic adventure of British climbing, bucking the boring obsession with micro-routes and sport climbing while at the same time not sacrificing technical levels of difficulty.

On Welsh slate, a combination of neck and ability helped him to play a major rôle in prolonging the new-route boom of the '80s. His reputation was cemented when he transferred his skills to the uncemented walls of Anglesey's sea-cliffs, where he made some extraordinarily worrying and hard routes in crumbling situations of alpine seriousness.

Unlike many of his peers, who single-mindedly sought the dubious benefits of career-plan sponsorship, Pritchard seemed happy to accept any remunerative crumbs that came his way as a by-product of his largely amateur activities. Instead he felt impelled to put adventure, pure and simple, at the top of his personal agenda. It is this, as well as his ability and laid back personality, which has maintained such a high regard and respect towards him amongst the hypercritical community of climbers.

Consequently, he began to embrace Scottish winter climbing and made one of those now rare transitions from high-standard crag climbing to the big mountains, expeditioning to big walls in Patagonia, Baffin Island, the Karakoram and Himalaya, as well as outlandish parts of Britain such as the Hebrides.

All this hectic activity was not without its price. Accidents and poor health dogged Pritchard, making his achievements and his continuing drive and enthusiasm all the more remarkable. Firstly he fell to earth in Gogarth's *Wen Zawn*, surviving the fall but almost drowning in a rock pool. Then came an impressive winter fall in Scotland which resulted in more hospitalisation. There followed a bout of a mysterious ME-type disease and on top of all this, he continued to suffer from altitude sickness on most of his Greater Ranges' expeditions. Surviving all of these setbacks is a major achievement by anyone's standards. Sadly, there was to be an even greater trial to come. After a blue riband year which had seen him make a full recovery and emerge triumphant with the Boardman-Tasker Prize for his brilliant first book *Deep Play*, a loose rock detached itself from a Tasmanian sea-stack while he was at its base and instantaneously robbed him of any satisfaction he may have gained from his achievements. His head took a direct hit and the terrible injury he sustained as a result has provided him with the biggest challenge of his life yet, but judging by his reaction to the calamity, and his powerful second book written in response, he is one of the few people capable of rising to it.

Paul Pritchard on a typically bold and technical slate route

else in the world. 'I'm only the fifth best climber on our street', was a famous quote of one major Sheffield-based climber of the era. Other hotspots where climbers congregated were dotted throughout the mountainous parts of the UK: Llanberis, Ambleside, Keswick, Fort William and Aviemore becoming most prominent.

The Battle of the Bolt

The spectre at the climbing feast throughout the decade was the increasing influence of the bolted climb, which had begun sprouting all over continental crags with alarming speed. Expansion bolts (fixed metal anchors which are permanently-affixed to blank rock which is unprotectable by any other means) had been around for many years, but their use had been extremely limited, partly due to ethical considerations, but mainly because of the difficulty of fixing the things in the first place.

By the '80s, however, the arrival of new highly portable cordless drills meant that it became relatively easy to place bolts. Continental climbers took to the new technology with gusto and soon many climbing venues were 'equipped'. The advantage of the new style of so-called 'Sport Climbing' was that it was safer – the bolts were less likely to pull out than traditional removable protection methods and allowed the climber to focus completely on the physical challenge of the climbing. In addition, much less equipment needed to be carried by the climber. Instead of the armoury of many wired chocks, Friends and other paraphernalia which weighed down the traditional climber like chain mail, a few karabiners were all that was needed to clip the rope through the *in situ*

bolt anchors. Even this exertion was reduced on harder routes by pre-placing the karabiners by abseil so that all that was required was for the climber to clip in the rope.

Many Britons now regularly climbed abroad on holidays and had sampled the instant gratification of equipped climbs. A degree of demand for a similar approach began to be voiced, triggering a philosophical (and sometimes physical) battle between pro-bolt and anti-bolt factions, reminiscent of the inter-war debate about piton use. Many feared the end of traditional climbing and the loss of the skills associated with it, such as self-reliance and route-finding judgement. These issues were less of a consideration on the Continent where there is far more climbable rock than in Britain, allowing scope for both types of climbing to co-exist. In the UK, with a much smaller finite resource, there remained a strong desire to 'conserve the adventure' of Britain's established routes which would be diminished by retrospective bolting. In addition, a majority of opinion favoured leaving challenges for future generations of bolder climbers on minimally protectable faces. The issues raised strong emotions, and pro-bolters frequently found their new protection points 'chopped', or removed, by opponents soon after their placement.

Although the debate is far from ended, blanket bolt-protection continues to be rejected by the majority as a suitable development on most British crags. In its place, a typically informal British consensus has evolved whereby most traditional crags are respected as bolt-free zones, but bolts are tolerated on some rock types, such as steep and overhanging limestone or quarried slate, where protection is otherwise very difficult or impossible to fix. Even in these

limited areas however, continental-style indiscriminate bolting is still frowned upon where 'natural' protection existed. Many British sport routes are therefore still rather challenging propositions compared with many of their continental counterparts.

The Rad Trads

Meanwhile, conventionally-protected climbing went from strength to strength. Partly in reaction to the bolt threat, a new generation of

Johnny Dawes tussles with typically rounded gritstone.
Break Dance (E3 6a), Stanage, Derbyshire

ultra-bold traditional climbers took standards of climbs to new heights. On gritstone and Welsh rock the athletic Johnny Dawes began making daring climbs requiring both extreme athletic ability and a very cool head. His innovative pioneering emphasised the folly of assuming that technical progress on formerly impossible blank looking rock required the addition of fixed protection.

Similarly, Paul Pritchard began questing across the unstable terrain of Anglesey's sea-cliffs, deliberately seeking adventure in its purest form. His description of his heightened state of consciousness during the lead of one of these daring ascents gives a flavour of their extreme seriousness:

> *"The first protection came after fifty feet of overhanging pocket-picking, taking care not to snap off the brittle edges. It was a briefcase-sized block detached on five sides and attached on its smallest end. Once looped it had to be laybacked and manteled. Monster spiders wait for prey at the roof. I pull by and gain a foot-cramping rest on a hanging porcelain slab a little higher… I gained height in convulsions. Classical music I'd heard in some car advertisement droned through my brain. I stopped being scared and, after an age of schizophrenic debate, I convinced myself that I could not fall off. I then began to look at myself rather than the rock. It was as though my body climbed while I gazed on…"*

The boldness had its price of course: Pritchard was later to take a bone-crunching ground-fall from 21m up on an Anglesey climb, narrowly escaping drowning from an incoming tide.

This is the **modern** world

The globalisation of climbing

(1990–)

A major change that affected the behaviour of British climbers in the last decade of the 20th century was the astonishing expansion of dedicated training facilities. Specialist climbing walls spread throughout the decade and became virtually ubiquitous in most major urban and climbing centres. This helped increase levels of participation still higher and raised climbing standards across the board like never before. The development of wall culture also had a large impact on the numbers and types of people taking up climbing. As facilities became more sophisticated, it became easier to introduce novices to safe virtual climbing in warm, dry, year-round venues. The numbers of people who at least had some experience of climbing rocketed, even if many of them did not venture much beyond centrally-heated facilities for their vertical adventures. In this way, the climbing scene took a further step in its evolution, away from being an élite, specialist pastime for enthusiasts, to one in which a wide range of people dabbled as just one more lifestyle option. This consumerisation of climbing, encouraged by the growth of the outdoor retailing market and related media, has led to the expansion of sponsored climbers whose familiar athletic bodies appear frequently in specialist magazines festooned in manufacturers' logos. The development of indoor climbing competitions, and recently, even ice-climbing competitions have also been driven by the same financial imperatives. However, in Britain at any rate, the hopes of big, money-spinning international competitions never really reached fruition. Instead a lower-key network of indoor bouldering leagues, local and regional competitions, and youth events has evolved which seems to suit the less-formal tradition of the British scene.

Another marked feature of the '90s has been a big expansion in the numbers of women taking up climbing. Although the macho barriers of the '50s and '60s were challenged by the likes of pioneering spirits such as Gwen Moffat and Brede Arkless, male domination of the sport only began to be seriously challenged in the '70s and '80s by climbers such as Jill Lawrence, Bonny Masson, Gill Kent and Gill Price, who made significant advances into the 'Extreme' grades. In the '90s women's climbing really came of age. Climbers like Glenda Huxter and Louise Thomas began operating at consistently

Below: Alison Hargreaves, one of Britain's foremost women mountaineers of the '90s, here pictured on *Right Unconquerable*, Stanage, Derbyshire

Above: Bizarre moves are *de rigeur* at indoor bouldering competitions. Problem setting has become quite a creative art
Left: 'Strong' Steve McClure on Johnny Dawes's *The Very Big and the Very Small*, Rainbow Slab, Llanberis

very high standards on rock while others such as Alison Hargreaves and Ginette Harrison achieved major mountaineering feats on Everest and Kangchenjunga, although sadly both died in the high mountains. More women than ever are taking up the sport in all its forms and it seems likely that this will expand enormously.

British climbing today encompasses a spectrum of sub-sports: traditional rock climbing, sport climbing, alpinism, mountaineering, bouldering, deep-water soloing, ice climbing, mixed climbing… the list is mind-boggling. Few people regularly indulge in all aspects, preferring to specialise in one branch or another. Climbers – always great travellers – now regularly take holidays abroad to sample many types of climbing as a specialised form of tourism. Popular venues include places as diverse as Spain, Thailand,

Leo **Houlding** (1980–)

Houlding first came to public prominence in 1996 when, as a 16 year-old, he made an audacious on-sight ascent of the extremely difficult and rarely accomplished *Master's Wall* on *Clogwyn Du'r Arddu*.

What made the feat even more startling was the fact that the cocksure teenager wore a pair of borrowed rock boots which were a size and a half too big for him. This eccentric devotion to baggy footwear was not new; Houlding had also on-sighted Gogarth's impressive hard climb *Conan the Librarian*, in a friend's re-soled pair of shoes which were three sizes too big. Houlding has continued his quest for bold and wacky climbs, such as his midnight ascent of the daunting Welsh climb *Lord of the Flies* by headtorch. Houlding's battery failed during the climb, necessitating a downclimb from the middle of the crux sequence to better holds from where he could lower a rope for a replacement battery and finish the route.

Should anyone begin to think that he was only interested in staging impressive stunts, Houlding assuaged any doubts about his motivation and ability by repeating a series of bold, cutting-edge routes in Britain and has carried his enthusiasm around the world, most notably to Eastern Europe, South America and the USA. It was in the US that Houlding rose to international prominence with his ascent of an extremely difficult big-wall climb in the

Yosemite Valley. Along with his frequent climbing partner Patch Hammond, Houlding climbed *El Niño*, a route that had only just been established by the German Huber brothers over a period of several weeks and declared the hardest long route in the world. The youngsters managed to repeat the 900m route in just four days with only one fall.

Pakistan, Peru, Vietnam, Australia and the USA. In the '90s climbing has started becoming a truly globalised activity.

Nevertheless, despite the momentous changes during the first century and a half of the sport, Britain largely retains its free-climbing, traditionally adventurous ethic. The amateur spirit lives on in the inspirational activities of many contemporary top performers. Tax-inspector Mick Fowler, for example, shows that in the age of the specialist even a non-professional can be outstanding in many types of climbing. His climbing record would be the envy of any pro, encompassing as it does first ascents of difficult rock and ice routes the length and breadth of the UK and of Himalayan, Russian and South American peaks. The latest generation of talented climbers is also showing both a healthy disregard for the reputations of fierce routes and the conventional strictures of career paths. 21-year old Leo Houlding, for example, has already proved impudent in the face of the cutting edge routes of the previous decade. He has climbed extremely difficult routes in Wales at night by torchlight for fun and also tilted at the toughest climbs in the USA – succeeding despite lacking experience of long, multiple-pitch big wall routes. Such antics suggest that despite all the commercial pressures, the creatively anarchic wellspring of British climbing is still bubbling vigorously.

It is probably true to say that if Walter Parry Haskett-Smith were to look down on the crags from the top of *Napes Needle* on the climbing landscape today, he would still be able to recognise the same sport that he helped kick-start with his audacious climb 115 years ago. One suspects he would nod approvingly.

Napes Needle

12
Mountain
Peoples

Research has shown that the heart rate of
a 33-year old Nepalese porter carrying loads
of 85kg (1.5× body weight) up to 3,300m is
comparable with that of a professional athlete

Nepal Himalaya
Sherpas, Tamangs, Rais and others

None of the mountaineering that has been undertaken in the Himalaya and Karakoram would have been possible without the co-operation of the indigenous peoples of the mountains. From the very first Victorian expeditions, the local inhabitants have been heavily involved in the quest to gain the highest summits, first as porters, then as fellow climbers.

The most famous tribe of mountain people in the Kingdom of Nepal are the Sherpas; a cultural grouping whose core homeland is the wild and spectacular high grazings of the Solu Khumbu. They have inhabited this highland zone of glacial valleys to the south of Everest for around 500 years, following a migration from eastern Tibet (their name, Sherpa, means literally 'east people'). In common with many remotely-situated and industrious people, the Sherpas became great travelling traders, roaming as far as Lhasa and to the plains of the Punjab. Indeed, such is their fame that many people assume that 'Sherpa' is a generic term for any mountaineering porter. However, the Sherpas are but one tribe of Nepalese mountain people whose lives are bound up with the uplands of their spectacular country. Others include the Tamangs, Thakalis, Rais, Limbus, Magars, and Gurungs.

Nevertheless, the Sherpas remain the most closely associated with the major Himalayan achievements of the past century and within mountaineering circles they have come to assume an élite grouping. Today Sherpas often hold key positions within trekking agencies and within expeditions. The upper hierarchy of Sirdar, Cook and high-altitude porters is more likely to be comprised of Sherpas than other Nepalese ethnic groups.

Couthy Scotsman Alexander Kellas was the first European really to appreciate the mountaineering qualities of the Sherpas. Until he began employing them after 1907 in preference to Swiss guides, they had been utilised solely as porters. Kellas recognised that the local knowledge of the Sherpas and their physiological adaptation to high altitude were far superior to imported European guides who were just as ignorant about Himalayan conditions as the clients. Kellas climbed with Sherpas extensively on his mountaineering expeditions in the Kangchenjunga region, which included the ascent of the fourth highest mountain climbed to that date, **Pauhunri** (7,065m).

But the Sherpas rise to fame in the eyes of the west really started with their association with the early Everest expeditions of the 1920s and '30s. Through books and films, they gained

Building work at the Rongbuk Monastery

Below: Load-carrying Sherpanis

Opposite: The view from the office window! Note the casual footwear.

Tibetan women

international fame. Thenceforth, Sherpas were often employed on exploratory mountaineering far away from their homeland such as on Tilman's and Shipton's Nanda Devi Sanctuary explorations. This expedition was also important in the evolving symbiotic relationship between western climbers and local people. For the first time the Sherpas were not taken primarily as servants, but as fellow climbers. One of the team was Tenzing Norgay, who would go on to partner Edmund Hillary on the first ascent of Everest in 1953.

The development of the modern trekking industry in the 1960s helped to secure the reputation of the Sherpas as the pre-eminent mountain experts in the Himalaya. Colonel Jimmy Roberts, a former Military Attaché in Kathmandu is usually credited with inventing the modern trekking industry in the 1960s. In order to realise his notion of holidays involving a tented progress through the Himalayan mountains, he required staff that were not only physically very tough, but also who possessed considerable initiative. Sherpas obviously fitted the bill, and their early association with the business has allowed them to dominate the management of this sector of the Nepalese economy. Today well over 75,000 people a year trek in Nepal, around a sixth of whom travel to see Everest via the Sherpa's Solu Khumbu

Above: Sherpa baby in a basket

Mani stones

Below: Market day in Namche Bazar, Nepal

homeland. However, these days, Sherpas are more likely to be involved in running trekking lodges and managing guiding agencies than carrying the loads of visitors along the trails. The trekking porters are more likely to belong to other Nepalese tribes, such as the Tamangs or the Rai. Sherpas, however, remain prominent in the rôle of climbing or high-altitude porters on expeditions, an occupation which is relatively well paid.

The tourist industry has also helped to replace sources of income within the Sherpa's Solu Khumbu homeland, which suffered as a result of the closure of traditional trading routes over the Nangpa La pass by the Chinese occupation of Tibet in 1950. Now, the Sherpas wait for buyers to travel to them, in the form of foreign visitors to whom they sell surplus expedition and trekking kit and food and lodging.

Tenzing Norgay Sherpa
(1914–1986)

The early life story of Tenzing Norgay is one of remarkable determination and self-belief. Starting off as a simple porter and ending up as a lead climber, over a period of nearly twenty years he made sure he was part of every expedition that tried to climb Everest.

His ambition began early. By the age of 18 he left his disapproving parents in the Sherpa homeland and journeyed to Darjeeling in India, where he hoped to be able to join one of the British expeditions to Mount Everest that were being organised there. Through dogged persistence, Tenzing got himself onto Eric Shipton's 1935 Everest Expedition and performed so well that he had no trouble in being hired on the following expeditions of 1936 and 1938. Unlike most of his fellow Sherpas of the time for whom, by and large, climbing was just a challenging way of making a living, Tenzing desperately wanted to get to the summit of Everest:

"For in my heart, I needed to go…
the pull of Everest was stronger for me than any force on earth."

His obsession was so great that he even participated in a clandestine 1947 trip through Tibet to the mountain with solitary Canadian climber Earl Denman, on the remote chance that even this might give him an opportunity to get to the top. He was back on a more conventional expedition in 1952 as climber with the Swiss, when he reached 237m short of the summit with Raymond Lambert.

By 1953, Tenzing had spent more time on Everest than any other human being, a fact of which the British were well aware in 1953. Tenzing was therefore one of the mainstays of their attack on the mountain. After his successful climb with Ed Hillary, Tenzing received many honours and was fêted, by world leaders and heads of state. He was invited everywhere and did much travelling. He became the first Field Director of the newly established Himalayan Mountaineering Institute, a post that he held for 22 years. When Tenzing died in 1986, the procession that followed his funeral bier was more than half a mile long.

Baltis and Hunzakuts
The indigenous mountaineers
of the Karakoram

To the west of the Himalaya, the great arc of giant Asian mountains continues in the form of the Karakoram range, a semi-desert landscape little affected by monsoon weather but possessing the most extensive glacier systems outside the polar regions. The area is also politically complex, straddling as it does the borders of Kashmir, Pakistan, China, Afghanistan and Tajikistan. K2, the second highest mountain in the world, dominates the central section of the range. Exploratory climbing here is most associated with the second great confederation of indigenous mountain people who are most often loosely referred to as Baltis, Hunzakuts and Nagars.

Baltis

Baltistan is an ancient kingdom situated in what is now northern Pakistan. The people are a mixture of Tibetans, Mongols, and other Islamic peoples of the northern Indus Valley united in their Shia Muslim faith and their language, which is a form of archaic Tibetan (partly for

Balti porters on the Baltoro Glacier

this reason, Baltistan is sometimes referred to as 'Little Tibet'). The capital, Skardu, is the gateway to K2 through which all expeditions pass *en route* to the village of Askole.

People from the Balti valleys of Skardu, Shigar, Basha and Haramosh have been employed as porters since the days of the earliest Victorian explorers. The pioneering expeditions of Sir Martin Conway and The Duke of the Abruzzi employed hundreds of local people to ferry their mountaineering and scientific equipment to K2 and the surrounding mountains in the late nineteenth and early twentieth century.

The energetic US mountain travellers Fanny and Walter Bullock-Workman also organised large caravans of porters during their major exploratory mountaineering expedition in 1903. Following a gruelling traverse of previously uncharted glaciated passes, their Balti porters

Balti porters

mutinied after being ordered to retrace their steps and cross to the Hispar Glacier *via* the difficult and dangerous Nushik La. Fanny later asserted that the refusal of the natives was due to 'cowardice and frequent desertion in the face of difficulties'. Given that locals often crossed crevassed passes without the security of ropes or ice-axes in search of gemstones and wild ibex, this seems likely to be far from the truth. Instead, contemporary critics of Bullock-Workman (such as the ebullient British Himalayan

Balti breakfast

veteran General 'Bruiser' Bruce), hint that her arrogant treatment of porters may have been the real reason behind her frequent industrial relations difficulties. The Bullock-Workmans, sadly, were not the last westerners to make the mistake of regarding local inhabitants merely as convenient baggage handlers and most famous episodes of trouble on Karakoram expeditions can normally be traced to such unreconstructed western attitudes.

Hunza and Nagar

The Hunza-Nagar Valley lies at the foot of **Rakaposhi** (7,788m) on a branch of the ancient Silk Road from China to Kashmir. The two ancient princely kingdoms of Hunza and Nagar existed here until historically recent times, fiercely independent of both outsiders and each other, despite sharing a language and ancestry. In the late nineteenth century, the British authorities to the south became fed up with constant raids by the Hunzakuts and Nagars on trading caravans, and suspicious of possible liaison between the region and Imperial Russia. In 1892 they subjugated the kingdoms by force. During the battle to take the Mir of Hunza's fort, the British Commander, Captain Algernon Durand, was surprised to be shot in the groin by a garnet bullet – standard issue among the resourceful Hunza riflemen of the period. The aggressive reputation of the Nagars lives on in their reputation as one of the more militant groups from which to recruit porters for expeditions to peaks accessible from the Hispar Glacier.

Overall, the portering and mountaineering infrastructure in much of the Karakoram is altogether less developed than in Nepal. It probably more resembles the early days of guiding in the Alps when subsistence farming was still the mainstay of most guides' livelihoods, supplemented by the occasional portering job as an additional, but welcome boost to income. Hunza provides an exception to this, being a place where the trekking industry is most developed and approaching levels of sophistication comparable with Nepal.

Indeed, within the Karakoram, Hunzakuts have perhaps acquired a reputation most similar to that of the Sherpas in Nepal as forming an élite grouping. (Hunza high-altitude porters were imported to Baltistan during Colonel Tony Streather's attempt on **Haramosh** (7,406m) in 1957 for example). Part of this is undoubtedly due to cultural attributes. The local Ismaili Muslim tradition adopts a more tolerant attitude towards dress codes and alcohol consumption than other parts of Pakistan, and Hunza itself prides itself on an independent spirit. Hunzakuts have perhaps more readily moved to take advantage of the business opportunities afforded by the influx of trekkers and mountaineers since the opening of the Karakoram Highway and relaxation of restrictions on access in the mid-1970s. It is perhaps no coincidence, therefore, that one of Pakistan's most famous mountaineers, (and the first Pakistani national to climb Everest and also K2 by a new route), Nazir Sabir, who has developed an internationally-renowned trekking agency and a mountaineering outfitters, is a Hunzakut.

Nazir **Sabir** (1955–)

Crossing a river of freezing cold glacial meltwater on the approach to **The Ogre**

Nazir Sabir was born in Hunza's Chupursan Valley in the very northern tip of Pakistan. From an early age he was always within sight and sound of some of the highest mountains in the world.

Following a college education, his passion for the lofty mountains dragged him back to pursue a career as a professional climber. Nazir is the only Pakistani to have climbed four of the five 8,000m peaks in his country and his ascents have always been accomplished with panache. He climbed **K2** (8,611m) in 1981 by a new route up the *West Face* with a Japanese partner, while the following year he ascended both **Gasherbrum II** (8,035m) and **Broad Peak** (8,047m) alpine-style with the South Tyrolean

Reinhold Messner and fellow Pakistani Sher Khan.

After taking time out to develop a trekking business Nazir climbed **Hidden Peak** (8,068m) in 1992 in just two days with fellow Hunza climbers Rajab Shah and Mehrban. Nazir has not only earned respect for mountaineering accomplishments however. In 1994 he was elected as Hunza's representative to Pakistan's Northern Areas Legislative Council and appointed adviser to the government on Education and Tourism, particularly trekking and mountaineering. Nazir has also been prominent in voicing concerns for environmental protection in the Karakoram and Himalaya

Read all about it!

Mountaineering and climbing magazines have evolved over time to suit the needs of a new breed of outdoor enthusiast

The present day **High Mountain Sports** has experienced 25 years' of publishing history that began with **Crags**, a bi-monthly rock-climbing magazine launched in February 1976.

Fun, rock climbing and irreverence were the hallmark of the original magazine, until commercial pressures took it to a wider audience and editorial base. With this came a title change to High in February 1982.

High is the UK's leading Climbing and Mountaineering magazine. Each issue features topical and authoritative articles on mountaineering, rock-climbing and advanced hillwalking worldwide. Superb colour photography complements quality writing by some of the most respected writers in the field.

An integral part of the magazine is Mountain Info, an international mountaineering information service edited by Lindsay Griffin, which is highly revered by climbers across the world.

The climbing world has changed dramatically from the first issue of Crags and as its readers' interests' change, so High has adapted to remain the key climbing and mountaineering publication in the UK.

To find out more look at
www.highmountainmag.com

ontheedge

OTE is Britain's liveliest climbing magazine, sticking its nose into all corners of our great sport – from sit down boulder starts to Himalayan expeditions – and sniffing out the latest gossip, news, profiles and features for where to go, what to do and what to say when you've been there! Featuring brilliant photography and the best writing, OTE sets a blistering pace – it's run by climbers for climbers.

To find out more head to
www.ontheedgemag.com

Summit

With the large increase in British Mountaineering Council membership, Summit was launched to help increase awareness and understanding about the issues that affect us, challenge our freedom as walkers and climbers and report on the policies that the BMC developed as a response.

Whether you are a dedicated mountain walker or a fanatical rock-climber, Summit provides information to help you enjoy your chosen activity.

To find out more look at
www.summit-mag.com

High Mountain Sports, On the Edge and Summit all continue to inspire and inform. They remain the essential read for mountaineers, climbers and serious hillwalkers

For more details on the range of climbing magazines available please contact

GreenShires Publishing, Telford Way, Kettering, Northants NN16 8UN.

Telephone: 01536 382500
Fax: 01536 382501
www.greenshires.com

Helly Hansen –
Technical Clothing = Performance = Exhilaration

'We want people to experience the exhilaration of the outdoor world, without worrying about things like wind, rain, heat or cold.'

Helly Hansen performance outdoor clothing combines the very ultimate in design, technology and innovation that allows people to experience the exhilaration of their chosen sport, to protect them from the elements and enhance their performance. Lightweight construction is less energy sapping, advanced materials allow breathability and keep out wind and rain. Innovative design gives maximum comfort. Each product is tried and tested in some of the fiercest conditions on earth, so whatever extremes you have to face you can be sure Helly Hansen has been there already.

Helly Hansen's authenticity lies in its heritage, it is one of the world's oldest outdoor brands. Nearly 125 years ago, Helly Juell Hansen, a Sea Captain in Norway, invented the world's first waterproof fabric, by rubbing linseed oil onto canvas. Realising the importance of his discovery and encouraged by the fact that sailors and fishermen could be protected from the elements, he started a company which has continued to lead and pioneer extreme weather clothing and is responsible for numerous 'firsts' in performance outdoor gear. At the World Exhibition in Paris, in 1878, Helly Hansen was presented with an award for innovation in waterproof fabric, an award which recognised the company's achievements at a very early stage in its growth and development. A copy of the award is on display at the National Mountaineering Exhibition, as testimony to the credibility that the company achieved even in its earliest days.

The company was encouraged by its early success, which drove the passion to take an even broader and more intensive view of fabric applications and their potential to protect individuals. Within the first five years of its development, Helly Hansen had sold 10,000 items of waterproof clothing and in 20 years this had risen to 60,000. The key to the company's success was intensive product testing which was applied to every new garment as vigorously as it is today. As demand for the products continued to grow, by the later 1890s, the company was exporting its waterproofs to Denmark and Sweden and many years later to England, South Africa and Chile.

Over the years, the company has diversified from producing work wear clothing, to sportswear. As the company continued to stay at the forefront of fabric technology, Helly Hansen identified the potential of creating products which would allow individuals to get the most from the outdoors, and enjoy their leisure activities to the full.

In 1961, Helly Hansen was responsible for the development of the very first 'pile' fabric and an example of the earliest design, as worn by **Doug Scott** during his expedition of the *South-West Face* of **Everest** will also be on display at the exhibition. These early garments formed the basis of research into the production of what is known today as the **Helly Hansen 3-layer system**, which consists of the famous **LIFA** base layer, fibre pile insulation layer and a waterproof breathable outer protection layer.

Before this Helly Hansen had been making inroads into waterproofing technology. In 1949, **Helox** was developed which was a very thin sheet of translucent PVC plastic sewn into waterproof coats and hoods. **Helox** soon became the 'must have' item for protective outdoor clothing and its popularity was evident in the 30,000 **Helox** coats which were produced each month at the factory's headquarters in Norway.

Another major breakthrough in technical clothing for the company came in 1975, when its now famous **LIFA** base layer was first launched. **LIFA** is a highly breathable base layer made from polypropylene which rapidly moves moisture away from the body and transports it to the surface of the fabric where it quickly evaporates. Since its early beginnings, **LIFA** has grown to become one of the world's most famous base layers and today the **LIFA** range is a high tech collection of underwear in varying weights for multi end usage.

Helly Hansen protects sailors, mountaineers, climbers, snowboarders, skiers, cyclists and walkers throughout the world. The company develops its clothing through feedback from its far reaching network of sponsored athletes.

These include **Mount Rainier** and **Courmayeur Mountain Guides**, **Paul Moores** and **Airlie Anderson**. The feedback from individuals and events alike, allows the company to continue to improve and develop its range into the preferred performance outdoor brand for athletes all over the world.

As well as hard-core events like the **Helly Hansen Three Peaks Yacht Race**, Helly Hansen recently supported an expedition to Bolivia. This involved a team of medical and science students measuring the effects of altitude sickness on the body at 5,200m. The students were given the **Helly Hansen 3-layer system** of dress to provide the ultimate protection in rapidly-changing mountain conditions.

Work wear still remains an important part of clothing produced by Helly Hansen today. Many outdoor jobs such as extreme offshore workers and fishermen benefit from Helly Hansen's knowledge and expertise to protect them from the harsh elements they're subject to as part of their everyday lives.

With the dawn of the new millennium, Helly Hansen has proved that it is still one of the strongest and most credible outdoor brands in the world. Today, Helly Hansen is a global company, represented in more than 20 countries with more than 500 product lines for men, women and children. It provides technical clothing for action sports and work wear in all seasons and the company continues to strive to be at the forefront of all the very latest advancements in design and technology. Because of its strong heritage within the outdoors, Helly Hansen will continue to innovate and experiment and test all of its products to the limit.

'Our product has been tried and tested in the most extreme conditions on earth. Helly Hansen has walked to the poles, climbed Everest, has survived the southern ocean in the fiercest of gales. However extreme the conditions you face, you can be sure Helly Hansen has been there already.'

Up *the* Wall

Climbing walls are here to stay, and whether they are a stepping stone for the 'real' world, big kids' playgrounds or physical training centres Entre-Prises can supply everything necessary.

Climbing has taken a little facelift over recent years. The crags have started emerging in places where there are aspiring and experienced climbers.

Climbing walls, as many diehard traditional climbers state, will never replace the real thing – the natural crag – but that has never been the intention. Climbing walls offer the user the opportunity to practice and perfect techniques that they can then adapt for use in the natural world, or they can be used as challenging keep fit arenas for which there is no tangible link to the great outdoors.

Entre–Prises have been producing and installing artificial climbing structures for over ten years. Initially climbing walls were simply rocks cemented into masonry walls but as expectations and technology have developed a broad range of climbing walls and boulders have emerged.

Entre–Prises produce over 600 climbing holds and five different climbing surfaces from wood based products through to fully sculptured Freeform. Leisure centres, climbing centres, youth groups, the Armed Forces and Schools have traditionally been the home for most developments but over recent years climbing walls have been built over swimming pools, on cruise liners, in theme parks, gymnasiums and shopping centres.

ENTRE PRISES
Climbing Walls

THE HELLY HANSEN
National Mountaineering Exhibition

The Helly Hansen National Mountaineering Exhibition

The **Helly Hansen National Mountaineering Exhibition** sited in Rheged, near Penrith, Cumbria, has been compiled with the help of many of Britain's best climbers – true experts in the history and heritage of a spectacular and challenging sport

Sir Chris Bonington leads the team and has contributed items from his own collection to enhance the exhibition displays

The result of all this hard work is a fascinating range of artefacts, a journey through time and a story that has never been told before. Many of the items to be seen, such as artefacts used by Mallory and Irvine on their Everest adventure, have never been on display until now.

The Exhibition

Britain has been at the forefront of climbing since the beginning of the **Golden Age of Alpine Climbing** in the mid to late 1800s, but the exhibition goes back further than that. The mysteries of the mountains are explored as the visitor takes a trip back in time to discover what lies behind the fascination mankind has always had with the world's high places. A series of Camps then tell the tale from the Alpine glory days through to the amazing achievements of the young 'mountain athletes' of today.

Visitors to the Exhibition are guided by the BBC's John Peel, who shares the highs and lows of a mountain expedition on their journey through the exhibition culminating in their own Everest experience.

The Exhibition is approached in spectacular fashion, over an aerial walkway suspended 10m above Rheged's main hall, although an alternative entrance is available for anyone not comfortable with the bridge. Julian Heaton Cooper's specially commissioned painting is on display in the hall. Measuring 3.9m by 2.1m, it is rendered in oils and took over two months to complete. It depicts climbing on **Scafell**, England's highest crag at 978m.

Moving through the lobby, the visitor comes to **A Splendid Adventure**. This circular room offers an incredible view of the roof of the world – the **Balloon Over Everest Panorama** taken by Leo Dickinson at 11,000m.

The **Tribute Gallery** is a portrait in words, paintings and photographs of some of Britain's all-time great climbers.

In **the Warehouse**, preparations for a large-scale expedition are under way. It is here that the visitor first meets the guide, John Peel.

The Walk In illustrates how climbing evolved into a sport, the impetus behind such activity and helps visitors understand how climbing became an end in itself.

In the **Abode of the Gods**, the mystical side of the mountains is evoked in images and sound. Ancient cultures of mountain peoples, their beliefs and mythology are beautifully illustrated.

The **Development of Climbing as Recreation** is a potted history of European climbing, outlined through artefacts, audio-visual sequences and fixed images, and is a thoroughly compelling story.

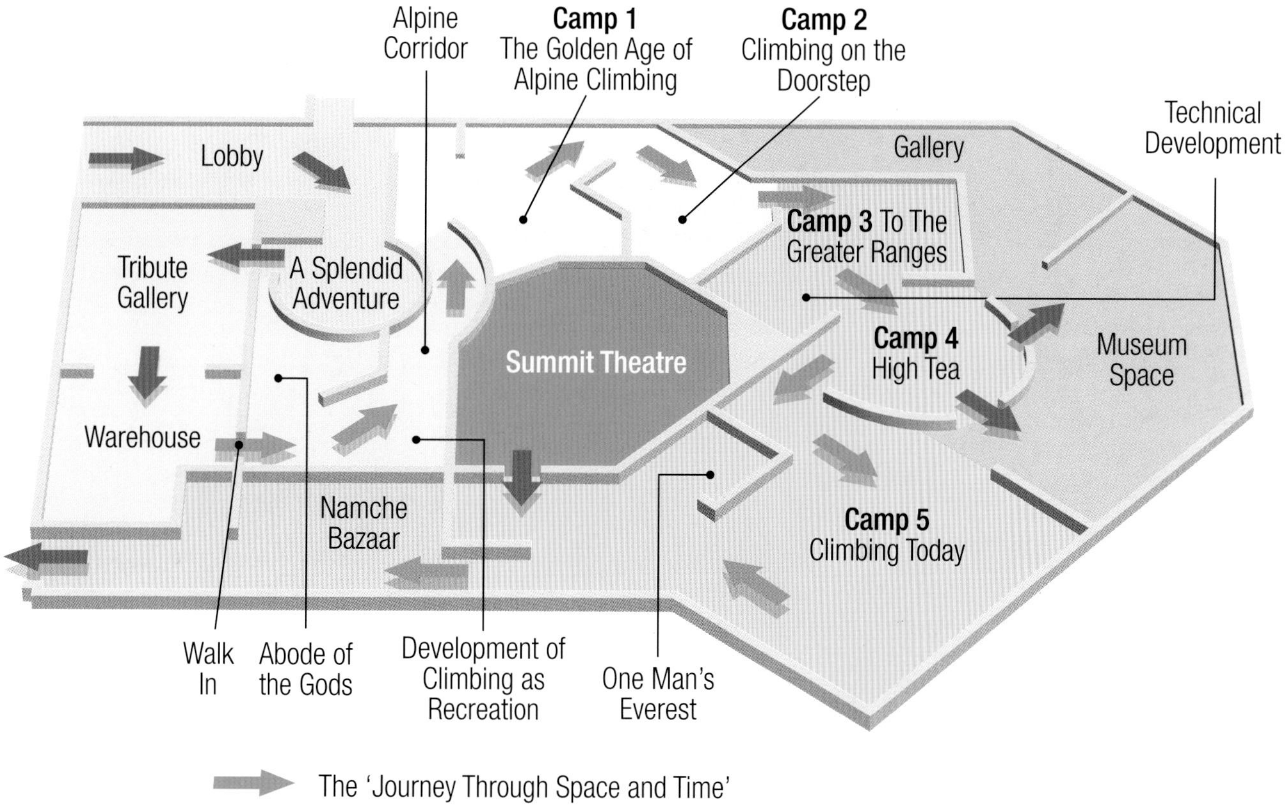

Diagram labels:

Alpine Corridor

Camp 1 The Golden Age of Alpine Climbing

Camp 2 Climbing on the Doorstep

Gallery

Technical Development

Lobby

Tribute Gallery

A Splendid Adventure

Camp 3 To The Greater Ranges

Summit Theatre

Camp 4 High Tea

Museum Space

Warehouse

Namche Bazaar

Camp 5 Climbing Today

Walk In   Abode of the Gods   Development of Climbing as Recreation   One Man's Everest

➡ The 'Journey Through Space and Time'

Further away in the Himalaya the visitor meets George Everest, Surveyor General of India who gave his name to the world's highest peak.

In **the Alpine Corridor**, the visitor steps back in time to an old English gentlemen's dining club where plans for great alpine conquests are being laid – the atmosphere of lamplight and the tinkling of raised glasses is brought to life as Albert Smith makes his first appearance.

Camp 1
the Golden Age of Alpine Climbing

This area covers the **Golden Age of Alpine Climbing**. Between 1854 and 1865 over 180 Alpine peaks were climbed for the first time, the majority of these by British climbers and their local guides.

The story of Albert Smith is told, the Victorian raconteur who did much to publicise the mountains through his music hall entertainments. This part of the Exhibition deals with the fascinating partnerships between 19th-century gentlemen Alpinists and the local experts hired as guides for their pioneering climbs.

The biggest prize in Alpine climbing became the **Matterhorn**. Getting to the summit of this charismatic peak became a race that drew international coverage in the press. The 19th Century newspapers took hold of the story and public support turned to outrage and horror. The Matterhorn prize was won by a British team led by Edward Whymper, as detailed in Chapter 2 of this book.

A copy of Whymper's own special design of tent is on display, along with the story of the man and his obsession.

Camp 2
Climbing on the Doorstep

A look at pre World War One climbing in Britain, featuring the work of England's first 'adventure photographers' – the Abraham brothers of Keswick.

Moving on to the 1930s, the growth of the Ramblers and the birth of the 'Cragrats' is charted. Cragrats was a term of endearment used by local farmers for the young climbers of this decade.

After World War Two, climbers rather than mountaineers came to the fore. These climbers broke socio-economic barriers and as transport became easier and cheaper, the door was wide open to a wide diversity of people.

Camp 3
To the Greater Ranges

This section of the exhibition covers major British successes in the Himalaya, including the '53 ascent of Everest. Other, less well-known, but equally successful climbs that were made by international teams are featured here.

The epic story of Mallory and Irvine is highlighted, as is the mystery surrounding their disappearance from high on Mount Everest.

Continuing through the tour, the visitor is appraised of the importance of **Technical Development**. John Peel, the 'Reluctant Mountaineer', dons the garments of the modern mountaineer to demonstrate how things have moved on thanks to scientific advances!

Sir Chris Bonington also joins in at this point to demonstrate how some of the more bizarre, technical items of equipment are put to use.

Camp 4
High Tea

George Band and Sir Chris Bonington talk to John Peel about their pioneering experiences on the mountains, the evolution of the sport and the brilliance of its future. Significant climbs on some of the world's highest and most difficult peaks are described in words and pictures by the climbers themselves.

Continued overleaf

the Organisers

Camp 5
Climbing Today

While the sport in Britain has its roots set firmly in the mountains, it has grown and spread out into a myriad specialised branches. Now there are many types of climbing and this spectacular array of images, coupled with interviews and film footage of the climbers of today. This section paints a clear picture of this amazing sport as it is practiced today. The visitor can also get hands-on experience of real climbing equipment.

The tour continues through **One Man's Everest**, George Band's private collection and the personal memories of the youngest member of the successful 1953 Everest ascent team. These are unique items, never before seen by the public.

To finish the tour of the Exhibition the visitor is invited into the **Summit Theatre**, a cosy, tented theatre showing a specially commissioned film. George Band tells John Peel how he became part of the '53 Everest expedition and what it was like. A personal account of an amazing historical event.

Finally, the visitor can browse around the display area, which displays a changing programme of exhibitions. These will range from key items representing the Mallory and Irvine collection to exhibitions of contemporary mountain art.

Visitors can buy a souvenir of their visit to the **Helly Hansen National Mountaineering Exhibition** at **Namche Bazaar**, which stocks a range of Fair Trade products crafted by the world's mountain people, as well as a range of such mementoes as posters, T-shirts, gadgets, mugs and so on.

MOUNTAIN HERITAGE TRUST

.BMC.

The **Mountain Heritage Trust**

The **Mountain Heritage Trust** is responsible for the **Helly Hansen National Mountaineering Exhibition**, making changes where necessary and keeping it up to date.

It also has a wider aim, as it works to find, record and preserve all aspects of British mountaineering heritage for future generations to enjoy. Pick up an Exhibition leaflet to find out more about becoming a **Friend of Mountain Heritage**.

For more information on the **Helly Hansen National Mountaineering Exhibition**, the **Mountain Heritage Trust** or the BMC call (0161) 445 4747.

Website: **www.mountain-heritage.org**

The **Mountain Heritage Trust** is a registered charity No. 1083219

The **British Mountaineering Council**

The **BMC** is a national organisation with over 53,000 members. It promotes the interests of climbers, hillwalkers and mountaineers and the freedom to enjoy their activities.

Through a democratic structure, the **BMC**:

- negotiates access improvements and promotes cliff and mountain conservation;
- promotes and advises on good practice, facilities, training and equipment;
- supports events and specialist programmes including youth and excellence;
- provides services and information for members.

Website: **www.thebmc.co.uk**

Photo **Credits**

Page	Position	Credit
OUTSIDE FRONT COVER		Chris Bonington Picture Library
INSIDE FRONT COVER		Chris Bonington Picture Library
VII		Chris Bonington Picture Library
VIII/1		Alpine Club/ Royal Geographical Society
2	U/R	The Wordsworth Trust
3	All	Etchings by Edward Whymper,
4	U/R	The Salkeld collection
	L/R	The Salkeld collection
5		John Cleare/Mountain Camera
6	L/R	Alpine Club
	U/R	*The Alpine Journal*, Vol. XXXII, February 1918
7	U/L	The Salkeld collection
	L/L	Etchings by Edward Whymper,
8	U/L	The Salkeld collection
	U/R	Alpine Club
9	All	The Salkeld collection
10	U/L	*The Matterhorn Disaster* by Gustav Doré, The Salkeld collection
	R	The Salkeld collection and Alpine Club
11	L/L	The Salkeld collection
	U/R	Alpine Club
12		Alpine Club
13		John Cleare/Mountain Camera
14		Chris Bonington Picture Library
15		Abraham Brothers*
16		Abraham Brothers*
17	U/L	Abraham Brothers*
	L/R	Fell & Rock Climbing Club
18		Fell & Rock Climbing Club

Page	Position	Credit
19		Colin Wells
20		Courtesy of Mrs Benstead
21	All	The Salkeld collection
22		Fell & Rock Climbing Club
23		John Cleare/Mountain Camera
24		John Cleare/Mountain Camera
25	U/L	The Salkeld collection
	L/L	Alpine Club
26		Steve Bell/Jagged Globe
27	L/L	The Salkeld collection
	U/C	Jim Curran
29	U/L	The Salkeld collection
	U/C	Steve Bell/Jagged Globe
30	U/L	Royal Geographical Society
	U/R	Royal Geographical Society
31		Steve Bell/Jagged Globe
32		The Salkeld collection
33		John Noel photographic collection
34	U/R	Royal Geographical Society
	L/R	The Salkeld collection
35		Alpine Club
36		T. Howard Somervell
37		Mrs Anne Russell
38	All	John Noel photographic collection
39	U/L	John Noel photographic collection
	L/L	John Noel photographic collection
	U/R	Noel Odell/Peter Odell
	L/R	Noel Odell/Peter Odell
40		Courtesy of Julie Summers

Page	Position	Credit
41		Chris Bonington Picture Library
42		John Cleare/Mountain Camera
43		Chris Bonington Picture Library
44/45		The Salkeld collection
46		Jim Curran
47		Chris Bonington Picture Library
48	U/R	John Cleare/Mountain Camera
	L/R	David Hamilton/Jagged Globe
49		Gordon Stainforth
50		Ken Wilson
52		Pinnacle Club collection
54		Chris Bonington Picture Library
55		Alf Bridge
56	L/L	Fell & Rock Climbing Club
	U/L1	Colin Wells
	U/L2	Colin Wells
57		Ian Smith
58		The Kirkpatrick collection
59		Chris Bonington Picture Library
60		John Noel photographic collection
61		Steve Bell/Jagged Globe
62		Morris Taylor
63		Chris Bonington Picture Library
65		Steve Bell/Jagged Globe
66	L/L	The Salkeld collection
	U/R	The Salkeld collection
	L/R	Royal Geographical Society
67	U/L	Royal Geographical Society
	U/R	Royal Geographical Society
	L/R	Stephen Goodwin/Jagged Globe
68		Royal Geographical Society
69		Chris Bonington Picture Library
70		John Cleare/Mountain Camera
71		Chris Bonington Picture Library
72	L/R	John Cleare/Mountain Camera

Page	Position	Credit
73	U/C	Derek Walker
	U/R	John Cleare/Mountain Camera
74		Jagged Globe
75		Chris Bonington Picture Library
76		Stéphane Pennequin/ Nuts Museum, Corsica
77	U/C	Chris Bonington Picture Library
	U/L	John Cleare/Mountain Camera
78	All	John Cleare/Mountain Camera
79		Chris Bonington Picture Library
80		Chris Bonington Picture Library
81		Chris Bonington Picture Library
82		Chris Bonington Picture Library
83	All	Chris Bonington Picture Library
84		Ron Holt/Jagged Globe
85		Chris Bonington Picture Library
86/87	All	Chris Bonington Picture Library
88		Chris Bonington Picture Library
89	L/C	Andy Cave
	U/R	Mick Fowler
90/91	Clockwise from left	Bill Birkett
		The Kirkpatrick collection
		Bill Birkett
		The Kirkpatrick collection
		Carl Ryan
		Bill Birkett
		The Kirkpatrick collection
92		Chris Bonington Picture Library
93	U/L	Ian Smith
	U/R	Geoff Birtles/ High Magazine archive
94	U/R1	Stéphane Pennequin/ Nuts Museum, Corsica
	U/R2	Wild Country
	L/R	Scarpa
95		Ian Smith

Page	Position	Credit
96	U/R	Ian Smith
	L/R	Glenn Robbins
97		Neil Foster
98		Ian Smith
99	U/L	Ben Lowe
	U/R	Ian Smith
100	U/C	Ian Parnell
	L/R	Fell & Rock Climbing Club
101		Steve Bell/Jagged Globe
102	All	Steve Bell/Jagged Globe
103	All	Steve Bell/Jagged Globe
104	All	Simon Lowe/Jagged Globe
105		Royal Geographical Society
106	All	Jim Curran
107	All	Jim Curran
108	U/L	Doug Scott
	U/R	Chris Bonington Picture Library
116		Chris Bonington Picture Library
OUTSIDE BACK COVER RIGHT		Chris Bonington Picture Library

© The publishers have made every effort to gain permission to use the photographs printed in this book.

If you have a query regarding copyright ownership of any photographs in this book, please contact:

The Mountain Heritage Trust,
British Mountaineering Council,
177-179 Burton Road,
West Didsbury,
Manchester M20 2BB.

Tel: (0161) 445 4747
Fax: (0161) 445 4500

www.mountain-heritage.org

The **Mountain Heritage Trust** is a registered charity No. 1083219

Index

A

Abraham Brothers 17–18, 56
Abruzzi, Duke of the
27, 30, 106
Aconcagua (6,959m) 25
aid (artificial) climbing 58
Aiguille des Grands Charmoz
(3,445m) 11, 13
Aiguille du Grépon (3,482m)
11, 13
Aiguille du Plan (3,673m) 13
Alpine Club 6, 9–11, 16,
27–30, 33
Alpine Journal 57
Alps, the 3, 13–14, 21, 26, 62,
73, 78, 80, 85
Andes, the 25
Annapurna 65, 81, 85
Annapurna I (8,091m)
65, 73, 81
Annapurna II (7,937m) 85
South Face 85
Archer Thomson, J.M. 22
Arkless, Brede 98
Armstrong, John 32
artificial aid pitches 77
Askole 48, 106
Assiniboine, Mt (3,610m)
24–25
Auden, John 46

B

Badrinath Range 43
Bagirathi III (6,454m) 55, 82
Baintha Brakk (7,285m) 85–88
Baltis 106

Baltoro Glacier 27, 46–48
Band, George 72, 80
Baxter-Jones, Roger 84
Beetham, Bentley 38
Bell, J.H.B. 52
Ben Macdhui (1,309m) 20
Ben Nevis (1,343m) 20, 22,
51–55, 74, 80
Point Five Gully 92
Zero Gully 92
Biafo Glacier 27
Bingley, William 2
Birkett, Jim 51
Black Shoot of Glas Maol 17
Boardman, Peter 81–84, 88
Bohren, Peter 6
bolt-free zones 97
Bonington, Sir Chris
72–73, 81, 85–88
Bourdillon, Tom 66
Bowfell Buttress 52
Braldu Glacier 46
Brazil, Angela 52
Bridge, Alf 51
Bristow, Lily 11, 13
Broad Peak (8,047m)
46–47, 108
Broad Stand 2, 19, 53
Brown, Joe 53, 58, 71, 80
Bruce, General Charles
27, 30, 34–36, 107
Bruce, Geoffrey 36
Budworth, Joseph 2
Bullock, Guy 36
Burke, Mick 81, 85

C

Canadian Rockies 20
Carrel, Jean-Anthoine 9, 25
Carrington, Rab 84
Caucasus, the 23–26
Cenotaph Corner 71
Chamonix 3–4, 71
Changabang (6,866m)
28, 83–84, 88
North Face 88
West Wall 83–84
Chimborazo (6,267m) 25
Cho Oyu (8,201m) 68
Clough, Ian 85
Coleridge, Samuel Taylor 1–2
Collie, Professor Norman
13, 20, 25, 30
Conway, Sir Martin 25–28, 106
Cordillera Real, Bolivia 25
Creagh Dhu 51, 74
Creagh Dhu Everest
Expedition 80
Cross, Sid 52–53, 56
Crowley, Aleister 22, 27–28
Croz, Michel 6, 9
Cunningham, John 74, 80
Curzon, Lord 33

D

de Vars Hazard, John 38
Dawes, Johnny 97–98
Dinas Cromlech 71
Douglas, Lord Francis 9
Dru (3,754m) 11, 85
Dunagiri (7,066m) 28, 82–83

E

East Rongbuk Glacier 36
Eiger (3,970m) 54–55, 83, 85
North Face (Nordwand) 55, 83
Elbrus (5,642m) 23, 24
'English air' 37
equipment 70
alpine rope 21
belay 56
camming device 94
chalk 94
crampons 56
expansion bolts 97
fell pole 21
grappling irons 70, 71
Hargreaves Nail 56
harness 76
ice-axe 21, 36, 43–44,
56, 74, 92
karabiners 70–71, 76, 97
kletterschuhe 57
nailed boot 21, 56
oxygen apparatus 36, 37
pitons 54, 57–58, 70, 77
plastic boots 94
rock shoe 94
ropes 76
slings 70–71, 76
Evans, Charles 66
Everest (8,850m) 30, 32–35,
40, 42–45, 55, 60–68, 80–88,
99, 105
base camp 80
British and Commonwealth
Everest Expedition, the
66, 80
Khumbu Icefall 80

North Col 36–39, 45, 60, 64
North East Ridge 36, 83, 88
Peak XV 32
South Col 67
South-West Face 81, 85, 88
West Ridge 62
Everest, George 32

F

Fawcett, Ron 95
Fell & Rock Climbing Club
50, 54
Finch, George 36–37, 40
Finsteraarhorn (4,274m) 35
Forbes, James 3–4
Fowler, Mick 88–89, 100
Freshfield, Douglas 24, 29

G

Garhwal Himalaya 28, 62, 82
Gasherbrum 46
Gasherbrum I (8,068m) 46
Gasherbrum II (8,035m) 108
globalisation of climbing 98
Golden Age 4–7, 24, 26
Graham, William Woodman
23, 28–29
Great Gable (899m) 16, 19, 50
Great Napes 19
Gregory, Alfred 66

H

Hadow, Douglas 9–10
Hall, Brian 84
Hamilton, Murray 93
Haramosh (7,406m) 107

Hargreaves, A.B. (Alan) 56
Hargreaves, A.T. (Albert) 54, 56
Hargreaves, Alison 99
Harrison, Ginette 99
Haskett-Smith, Walter Parry
16, 19, 20, 21, 100
Hastings, Geoffrey 13, 30
Haston, Dougal 81, 88
Herford, Siegfried 22, 50
Hidden Peak (8,068m) 84, 108
Hillary, Sir Edmund
40, 66–68, 103
Hinks, Arthur 34, 36, 37
Hispar Glacier 27, 48, 107
Houlding, Leo 100
Howard-Bury, Charles 34, 36
Hudson, Charles 9
Hunt, John 65, 66
Hunza 48, 107
Huxter, Glenda 98

I

Inglis Clarke, Charles 52
Inglis, H.D. 3
Irvine, Andrew 'Sandy'
35, 38–40, 60
Italian Alpine Club 9

J

Jannu (7,710m) 84
Javelin Blade 51
Johnson, Dr Samuel 2
Joint Himalyan Committee,
(*see* Mount Everest Committee)
Jones, Owen Glynne
17–18, 20

Jotunheimen 24
Jungfrau (4,158m) 3
Junior Mountaineering Club
of Scotland 54

K

K2 (8,611m) 27–30, 46–47,
65, 83, 106–108
Kabru (7,316m) 28
Kamet (7,756m) 37, 62
Kangchenjunga (8,586m)
28, 88
Karakoram 25, 27, 33, 42–48,
75, 96, 102, 106–108
Kellas, Alexander 29–30,
36–37, 102
Kelly, Pat 52
Kennedy, Edward Shirley
5–6
Kennedy, Thomas 6
Kent, Gill 98
Kenya, Mt (5,199m) 42, 44
Kern Knotts Crack 16, 17
Kirkus, Colin 51, 55, 56, 82
Kongur, Mt (7,719m) 83, 85

L

le Blond, Lizzie 11
Lake District 2, 17, 20–22, 43,
50–51, 54, 57
Lawrence, Jill 98
Leslie Stephen 6
Lester, W.R. 17
Linnell, Maurice 55
Livesey, Pete 93
Llanberis 3, 71, 95
Longland, Jack 51
Longstaff, Tom 28, 36, 43, 64
Lowe, G.T. 19, 66

M

MacInnes, Hamish 80, 85, 92

MacIntyre, Alex 84
Macphee, Graham 51–52
Mallory, George Herbert Leigh
30, 34–40, 60
Marshall, Jimmy 74
Masson, Bonny 98
Matterhorn (4,479m) 3, 5–9,
12, 25
East Face 9
Hörnli Ridge 10–11
Zmutt Ridge 13
McDonnell, Lady Evelyn 11
Menlove Edwards, John 57
Mer de Glace 3, 14
Mickledore 2, 19, 57
Millstone Grit 71
Moffat, Gwen 77, 98
Mont Blanc (4,807m) 3–4,
13–14, 62
Mont Pelvoux (4,103m) 8
Moore, Adolphus 6, 24
Morley, John 33
Morshead 36
Mount Everest Committee
34, 37–40, 55, 62, 64–65
Mumm, Arnold 33, 37
Mummery, Albert Frederick
11–13, 20, 22, 24, 29–30, 82
Munich Tactics 58
Murray, Bill 52, 56
Mustagh Pass 33
Mustagh Tower (7,273m) 46

N

Nagar 107
Nanda Devi (7,824m)
41, 43, 45, 46
Nanda Devi Sanctuary
28, 43, 103
Nanga Parbat (8,125m)
13, 30, 65, 82, 88
Diamir Face 30

Napes Needle 16, 18–19,
28, 100
Nelson, Alice 52–53, 56
Nepal, Kingdom of
32, 64, 102
Nicholson, Ian 92
Nimlin, Jock 51
Nisbet, Andy 93
Noel, John 33–34, 36, 39, 60
Norgay Sherpa, Tenzing
40, 66–68, 103, 105
Norton, Edward 36–38, 61
Noyce, Wilfrid 66
Nunn, Paul 92
Nuptse (7,841m) 85

O

Odell, Noel 38, 39, 40, 46
Ogre, The
(*see* **Baintha Brakk**)
Old Man of Hoy 78
Oppenheimer, Lehman 20
Orion Face Direct 74
Outdoor Education
Centres 75
Outram, James 25
Outward Bound 75

P

Paillon, Mary 11
Pamir, the 33
Patey, Tom 74–75
Pauhunri (7,128m) 29–30, 102
Peak District 22, 51, 73
Peascod, Bill 52
Perrin, Jim 66
Petit Dru (3,730m) 71
Pidgeon, Anna & Ellen 11
Pilley, Dorothy 52
Pinnacle Club 52
Piz Palu (3,908m) 11
Popocatépetl (5,452m) 28

Price, Gill 98
Pritchard, Paul 95–96, 98
Pugh, Dr Griffith 66
Puttrell, J.W. 22

R

Raeburn, Harold 34, 36
Rais 102–104
Rakaposhi (7,788m) 107
Redhead, John 91
Renshaw, Dick 82–83, 88
Richardson, Katy 11
Rishi Ganga Gorge 28, 43
Roberts, Colonel Jimmy 103
Rock & Ice 71
Rouse, Alan 84
Royal Geographical Society
33–34
Rubicon Wall 54
Ruskin, John 3–4
Ruttledge, Hugh 46, 55,
60–62

S

Sabir, Nazir 107
Saunders, Victor 88
Scafell (963m) 19, 22,
51–53, 55, 57
Central Buttress 22, 50,
52–53, 57
East Buttress 51, 55
Scafell cliff 19
Scafell Crag 22
Steep Gill 22, 52
Scafell Pike (977m) 2, 19
Scott, Doug 81, 84–88
Scottish Mountaineering
Club 22, 52, 54, 74
Selkirk Range 24
Shaw, George Bernard 36
Sheffield Climbing Club 51
Sherpas 29, 102, 107

Shipton, Eric 42, 45–46,
60–67, 82, 103, 105
Shishapangma (8,027m) 84
Sikhdar, Radhanath 32
Slingsby, Cecil 13, 24
Smith, Albert 3–4
Smith, Robin 74
Smythe, Frank 42, 60–62
Snowdon (1,085m) 3, 51
Clogwyn Du'r Arddu
51, 55, 78, 100
Great Slab 51
Snowdonia 2, 22, 51, 71
Solu Khumbu 102
Somervell, Howard 36–38
Spantik (7,027m) 88
Golden Pillar 88
Spence, Kenny 93
Spender, Michael 46
sport climbing 96–99
Stobart, Tom 66
Straton, Isabella 11
Streather, Colonel Tony 107
Syrett, John 93

T

Tamangs 102–104
Tasker, Joe 82–84, 88
Taugwalder 9–10, 78
Terrordactyl 92
Thomas, Louise 98
Tibet 32, 64
Tilman, Harold William
42, 44–45, 48, 64, 82, 103
Towers of Paine (2,799m) 85
Trango Towers (6,286m)
46–47
Trisul 37
Tryfan (917m) 57
Tyndall, John 6, 8, 9

U

Unsworth, Walt 4

V

Via Tak (3,900m) 26

W

Wager, Lawrence 61
Walker, Lucy 11
Waller, Ivan 51
Ward, Michael 66
Warren, Charles 82
Wasdale 16, 22, 28
Wasdale Head
13, 17, 22, 28
Wasdale Head Hotel 19
Wast Water 17
Weisshorn (4,506m) 8
Westmacott, Mike 66
Wheeler, E.O. 36
Whillans, Don 53, 71–73,
81, 85
Whymper, Edward 8–10,
12, 21, 25
Wilson, Ken 74
Winthrop Young, Geoffrey
22, 34–35
Wollaston, Dr 36
Wordsworth, William 2
Wylie, Charles 66
Wyn-Harris, Percy 42, 61

Y

Younghusband,
Sir Francis 32

Z

Zermatt 3, 6, 9, 10
Zinalrothorn (4,221m) 11